Empowered by Data

Empowered by Data

How to Build Inspired Analytics Communities

By
Eva Murray

WILEY

Published by John Wiley & Sons, Inc., Hoboken, New Jersey.

Published simultaneously in Canada.

For general information on our other products and services or for technical support, please contact our Customer Care Department within the United States at (800) 762-2974, outside the United States at (317) 572-3993, or fax (317) 572-4002.

Wiley publishes in a variety of print and electronic formats and by print-on-demand. Some material included with standard print versions of this book may not be included in e-books or in print-on-demand. If this book refers to media such as a CD or DVD that is not included in the version you purchased, you may download this material at http://booksupport.wiley.com. For more information about Wiley products, visit www.wiley.com.

Library of Congress Cataloging-in-Publication Data:

Names: Murray, Eva Katharina, 1985- author.
Title: Empowered by data : how to build inspired analytics communities / by
  Eva Murray.
Description: Hoboken, New Jersey : Wiley, [2021] | Includes index.
Identifiers: LCCN 2020032115 (print) | LCCN 2020032116 (ebook) | ISBN
  9781119705659 (paperback) | ISBN 9781119705697 (ePDF) | ISBN
  9781119705703 (ePub)
Subjects: LCSH: Business enterprises—Technological innovations. |
  Business—Data processing. | Organizational effectiveness—Data
  processing.
Classification: LCC HD45 .M865 2021 (print) | LCC HD45 (ebook) | DDC
  658.4/038—dc23
LC record available at https://lccn.loc.gov/2020032115
LC ebook record available at https://lccn.loc.gov/2020032116

Cover image: © Samuel Parsons
Cover design: Wiley

Printed in the United States of America.

SKY10021513_092920

Contents

Foreword

Do you remember your first career-related cause?

Do you remember the first time in your business career when some issue, some topic, some concern grabbed you and didn't let go? Some people remember the first time they encountered an unfair human resources decision. Or when they helped turn around an unhappy customer. For so many of you reading this book, what comes to your mind is likely what comes to my mind: the joy of data. Or, more specifically, the discovery that you love data and you want others to love data too.

Maybe you want your colleagues to understand the importance of a question well asked—and well answered. Or you want to bring together people around the idea that data can build better processes, better companies, and better work environments. And maybe most critically, you want to bring teams together to find smarter ways to have happier, more satisfied customers. You want to inspire others with data the way that data have inspired you. You want to create meaningful connections that have impact on people's lives.

This is the book for you. This is the book that will help you bring those people together in a community that's more than just shared interests. Eva Murray has written you a book that will help you build a successful community. Not just a user group, your community will be one of collaborative relationships, inspirations, and aspirations.

I was lucky—I joined Tableau Software (now a Salesforce company) as head of marketing when the company had just a few thousand users. Eleven and half years later when I left, the company had millions of users across its multiple products, including Tableau Public. It's because of the growing, evangelical, and inclusive communities of people using data that the company became so successful.

And no one is a better example of what it means to build an inclusive community than Eva. She's had an incredible journey, building a huge data community of data enthusiasts and defining the path for how to bring them together. Her advice and insights in this book are unparalleled. They're not only smart but practical. Motivating and guiding the development of a community is hard work, but Eva has written you a roadmap that will have you feeling confident, supported, and prepared.

So, follow Eva's advice. But follow it only if you want to have an impact, build better businesses, and, most important, help and inspire people around you. Follow it because you want to start a cause—your personal cause of building an influential community that lives and breathes data.

Elissa Fink

May 2020

Acknowledgments

This book started as a 15-minute presentation at the Wharton People Analytics Conference 2019 in Philadelphia and grew over the following months into a firm idea, then a proposal, and finally the book you are holding in your hands.

There are a number of people who were part of that process, and I want to thank them and acknowledge their contributions to this project.

First and foremost, thank you, Andy, for your unwavering support, your help and feedback and for being by my side. Thank you for reminding me to take breaks, for giving me the space to write and for celebrating with me when it was done. I learned so much from you about making valuable contributions to the communities I am part of and it helped me become the community builder I am today. I am very fortunate to have you in my life!

Thank you to our #MakeoverMonday community and the wider Tableau and analytics community. I love being part of these networks and being connected to all of you, helping you learn and learning from you in return. Dozens of people in these communities have shaped my path over the last few years and I am ever grateful that you did, because you gave me the opportunity to work in an industry and a job I love, making a difference in people's lives.

Thank you to Marian who patiently and diligently read through this entire book, giving me feedback and listening to my questions and concerns. I'm lucky to have you as a friend and look forward to each of your visits to London.

Thanks also to every single person who said yes to having their story feature in this book. I loved finding out more about the communities you run and are part of and to work your stories into these pages so others can be inspired, learn from your journeys and connect with you. You helped me make the suggestions, recommendations, and ideas in these chapters become relatable and real. So Meera, Zunaira, Samo, Ash, Elizabeth, Sarah C, Pippa, Diego, Emily, Pascal, Fi, Simon, Maria, Sarah B, Natasha, Louisa, Caroline, Sam, Joe, Paul, and Katie: Thank you!

Of course, no book is complete without an editor and a publisher. Purvi and Bill, it has been an absolute pleasure to work with you once again on a book for the data analytics market. I appreciate your expertise and professionalism, your swift responses to my questions, and the calmness that you brought to this project. Thank you for all your help along the way.

PART I

Chapter One

If You Want a Data Culture, Build a Community

When you picked up this book, you were likely looking for an alternative solution to building your data culture, for suggestions beyond selecting the "right metrics" and building a good relationship with your chief data officer.

There are many reports out there about building a data-driven culture for your enterprise, plenty of "10 steps" lists and surveys resulting in recommendations. Those suggestions can be helpful in establishing a data culture, but the missing ingredient is the *human* element.

Having worked with thousands of analysts across the world and through my conversations with organizations, I have found that the most effective way of establishing a data culture within your business is to start by building a community.

And that is what this book will deliver for you: thoughts and ideas behind analytics communities. We will explore what they are, what they can look like, how they operate within organizations, and how you can set up your own community. After a few chapters, you will have enough information to get started. You will read about people who have started data communities within their organizations and what made their communities successful. You can take the suggested activities, events, and initiatives in the second part of the book, combine them with the templates provided, and start building your community today.

Why Do Organizations Aim to Become Data-Driven?

In Gartner's Fourth Annual Chief Data Officer Survey (2018), more than a third of all respondents (36%) stated that having a data-driven culture in the organization was *critical* to the success of data and analytics teams. Gartner's report further sees the responsibility for establishing a data-driven culture with the chief data officer.[1]

The *Harvard Business Review* agrees with this sentiment, stating that a data-driven culture must be initiated and driven by the people in top management.[2]

Leading analytics software firm Tableau considers culture the missing link for success in an environment where data are strategic assets for many organizations.[3]

Clearly, there is something beyond collecting and analyzing data, something that requires not just a significant shift in the collective mindset of your employees but also in the approach taken to the concepts of data literacy and data democratization. Extracting value from your data requires more than having a select few people work with the data to generate information and insights. Organizations are increasingly embracing data and the insights they contain, helping them arrive at better decisions that improve processes, products, services, and actions.

While the media may suggest that robots and AI are about to take over the world, most organizations are not quite there yet. Many businesses rely

---

[1]Mike Rollings, Alan D. Duncan, Valerie Logan, "10 Ways CDOs Can Succeed in Forging a Data-Driven Organization," Gartner, May 22, 2019,
https://www.gartner.com/doc/reprints?id=1-1OBMC46L&ct=190726&st=sb
[2]David Waller, "10 Steps to Creating a Data-Driven Culture," *Harvard Business Review*, February 6, 2020,
https://hbr.org/2020/02/10-steps-to-creating-a-data-driven-culture.
[3]Tableau, "Data Culture: Your Missing Link to Thriving in the Data Era," nd,
https://www.tableau.com/en-gb/data-culture

heavily on spreadsheets and manual processes; even though there is clearly a shift to more sophisticated systems and tools, the shift is still very much a work in progress.

Nevertheless, organizations across different industries, geographies, and sizes are using data to improve their decision making. They are progressing from understanding what happened in the past toward predicting what will happen in the future. The more data they collect and analyze, the more their questions evolve and the more their demands for improved analyses, more sophisticated predictive models, and more data-driven decisions increase. As a result, organizations require more sophisticated analytical skills among their people.

What Does Data Give Us that Experience Cannot?

Those of us who have gained experience over time might be tempted to ignore data and go with what our intuition, our gut, tells us. And in businesses across the world, there are many situations in which decision makers act based on their experience rather than on hard facts.

Sometimes there are no data available. Sometimes the decision is too urgent; it cannot wait for analysis and its results. And sometimes the decision makers think they know best and there is no need to query the data.

However, there is so much value in the data, and there are things we might not be able to see or know from just experience or observation. Take, for example, a soccer match. You are the coach and your team is playing. Every player wears a tracking device that captures their position on the pitch, measures their heart rate, and calculates their acceleration. These data give you insights for each athlete, specific to their position, so you know how many dives your goalkeeper made and in which direction to prevent the opponent from scoring.

Throughout the match, these data mean you know exactly how far your players have run, at what speeds, what their heart rates are, and how they compare to their training or other matches they have played.

Based on experience, when you look at your right winger, you are confident that she can play the entire game and perform at the expected level. But the data might tell you otherwise. You might see, based on the tracker in her shoes, that her running has become unbalanced, favoring one leg, potentially a sign of fatigue. With 20 minutes left to play and a substitute player available, will you rely on your gut feel and observation or trust the data and decide to make the substitution, to give your athlete a rest and perhaps prevent her from sustaining an injury?

In high-performance sports in particular, where the relationship between athletes and their coaches and the dynamic in the team require constant interaction and feedback, experience is paramount. From my own experience as a triathlete, I can attest to the value of having an experienced coach who can see and notice what we as athletes might not even be aware of. Yet, even in sports, with a long history and with outstanding expertise among coaches, data are making a big difference: from helping athletes improve their performance, to helping coaching teams develop new ideas for their game strategy, and to driving interactions with fans and pundits.

Our experience and instincts, as well as our observations, will always be limited and somewhat subjective. Acknowledging these limitations and becoming open to the use of data to make us better in what we do means we can make better decisions for the organizations we work for, the teams we work in, and the customers and communities we serve.

What Does a Data-Driven Culture Look Like?

Data culture is not necessarily something that follows a neat checklist, but rather it involves the general acceptance and use of data in driving decisions at every level, in coming to conclusions, in testing hypotheses. Having a data culture means data are accessible to employees across the organization, whether they are tasked with developing a marketing campaign, creating a new product, implementing a sales strategy, or recruiting new employees. When data are at the heart of everything the organization does, people will ask "What does the data tell us?" before engaging in fruitless discussions and arguments in which one person's experience stands against another person's experience.

Merely saying that data and analysis are important and just encouraging people to become data literate and data-driven is not enough. Data need to be truly accessible, need to be made visible, and need to be communicated effectively. Every major decision needs to be substantiated by data in order to be meaningful, and doing that requires transparency and proactive communication to build trust across the entire organization.

And when people have been granted access to the data and have been asked to address questions using data, they also need to have the right tools to analyze the data, find insights, turn them into information that decision makers can act on, and be able to share the outputs with the right people. To be most effective in their work, analysts and businesspeople working with data will need to be trained, must have their skills enhanced as they carve out their own expertise within the organization, and must be able to collaborate with others.

This is where community comes in and becomes the support structure for your data culture.

Forming a data-driven community in your organization gives you the collective intelligence of your people and an opportunity to reduce or even remove silos, to increase collaboration, to raise the quality of analytical outcomes, and to drive engagement.

To shape your own data-driven culture, I recommend that you bring together the people who will become key influencers in such a culture—the people already working with data, running analysis, producing reports, and sharing insights. Use them as catalysts to create a data-driven mindset more generally in your organization, even with the people who currently do not use data in their day-to-day work. At some point they will. They will have to; it is inevitable. And your analytics community is the support structure you need to turn every one of your people into an analyst, a curious, inquisitive person who constantly asks "What do the data say?"

Chapter Two

What Is an Analytics Community?

You are probably familiar with a number of communities around you—perhaps local sports clubs, a religious institution, or the physical community where you live. Now think about an analytics community; how does it differ from other communities we may know, and what are the similarities?

It's probably easiest to start with the similarities, highlighting those characteristics that can be found in most communities you encounter. In analytics communities, like-minded people come together around the topic of analytics, and they likely form interest groups for various subtopics, such as data engineering, data visualization, and communicating with data.

The most common trait of the many analytics communities I have encountered is that they all started with one or a few people who were passionate about data and analytics and who made it their goal to grow their own skills and those of the people around them while fostering a data culture in their organization.

Analytics communities come in all shapes and sizes, just like the organizations they are part of.

One such community I want to introduce you to has formed around the social data project #MakeoverMonday, which I cohosted with Andy Kriebel from 2017 to 2019 and that I now run with Charlie Hutcheson. How did the #MakeoverMonday community come about? How did it grow? What does it look like today? Along the way, we, the people leading #MakeoverMonday, learned a lot of lessons, lessons we will dive into in more detail in Part 2.

#MakeoverMonday, the Social Data Project that Changes Visualizations and Lives

#MakeoverMonday had its humble beginnings as a weekly exercise that Andy Kriebel, Tableau Zen Master and Head Coach at The Data School, did purely for his own learning and development. Having read a number of books on data analysis and visualization, he decided to set himself a weekly challenge to create a makeover, or improved visualization, of a chart he found online. He would select a chart, find the data for it, and create a visualization that better represented the data and information.

Over the course of three years, this habit helped Andy learn more about data visualization best practices, hone his Tableau skills, and practice different visualization techniques while tackling a different topic each week.

In 2016 Andy was joined by Andy Cotgreave of Tableau, and the two Andys turned #MakeoverMonday into a project that anyone could join. They published the data sets online each week and shared their thoughts and approaches as well as their makeovers on their respective blogs.

In 2017 I took over from Andy Cotgreave. The project had become a success in the Tableau and the wider data visualization community with hundreds of participants and well over 3,000 visualizations created in 2016 alone. Together, Andy and I grew the project further, with well over 2,000 people joining the project in the following years.

We added new elements to the weekly schedule to provide additional learning opportunities for our participants.

- We started with a weekly webinar series called Viz Review, during which we provide feedback to participants by critiquing their visualizations and showing them what to change and how to go about it.

- We ran additional webinars with community members and external experts to broaden the range of ideas coming into this community.
- We wrote weekly blogs with lessons learned from each challenge and turned them into a book, which we published in 2018 with the title *#MakeoverMonday: Improving How We Visualize and Analyze Data, One Chart at a Time.*
- We captured our favorite visualizations from each week in a recap blog post to highlight the great work done by our participants.
- We ran dozens of live events in Europe, the United States, and Australia to bring together a community of people who typically only interact online via Twitter.

Characteristics of the #MakeoverMonday Community

#MakeoverMonday is a social data project that happens online and brings people together virtually around our mission to improve the way we visualize and analyze data—one chart at a time. With that in mind, a lot of the communication happens via Twitter, which provides the project with a platform where people can easily share their work, ideas, and feedback while also affording participants visibility in the wider community and various industries.

For us, keeping #MakeoverMonday as open and accessible as possible is very important, so that people can share their work, showcase their skills, and be noticed by others. Such accessibility has helped many participants when it comes to networking, finding new job opportunities, and connecting with like-minded people.

Now we look in more detail at the specifics of this project.

Aside from running the project online and making it easy to access, there are five pillars that #MakeoverMonday is based on:

1. Develop your skills.
2. Build your portfolio.
3. Learn and inspire.
4. Grow your network.
5. Have an impact.

Know what we want folks to get out of the community, and what we want the community to create.

weekly challenge, new topic each week.

provide feedback

1. Develop Your Skills

The weekly data visualization challenges we give the #MakeoverMonday community provide an exercise for users to hone their technical skills and their understanding of best practices and design concepts. These challenges offer a fresh topic every week. Continuous and consistent practice can only make you better, and #MakeoverMonday gives people the platform to improve each week and learn from others.

We have been privileged to follow the journey of many participants and to see their skills grow and improve. The most consistent community members, those who tackle challenges regularly over an extended period of time, are typically those who reap the biggest rewards. Their beginnings are often characterized by finding their way into weekly participation, developing their own style and a deeper understanding of best practices. After a few weeks, their skills tend to improve markedly, producing consistently good work, showing their insights clearly, formatting their visualizations effectively, and having a clear message.

None of this development happens by accident or overnight. And our way of ensuring that people can build their skills and expertise in data visualization is to provide constructive feedback. We found giving feedback to hundreds of people each week is impossible. So, in 2017 Andy and I developed a feedback webinar that streamlined the process.

Each week participants who would like their visualizations reviewed by us opt into the feedback process by using the hashtag #MMVizReview on Twitter when submitting their work.

Every Wednesday Charlie and I run this webinar and work through the submissions. Typically, we can provide feedback on around 20 submissions during the 60-minute live webinar. A recording of the webinar is available shortly after for those unable to view it live.

The webinar is the most effective way for us to give feedback as we can talk through our comments and convey our critique using our tone of voice, which we have found to be easier for people to receive than multiple short and sharp tweets. So much of the tone of communication can get lost in social media messages; that is why we maintain the webinar process diligently.

Additionally, we can share content from our computers to support our explanations and critiques. We can interact with visualizations, ask questions, and provide suggestions. We often run short demonstrations of the changes and updates we suggest to participants to show them that our suggestions will not be time consuming to implement and to highlight the effect of making those changes.

2. Build Your Portfolio

A key aspect for #MakeoverMonday is that it gives participants the opportunity to build a portfolio of their data visualizations, showcase their skills, and highlight their style and analytical abilities.

Someone who is just getting started in their career and wants to work with data and visualizations has the opportunity to create 52 Makeovers over the course of a year, tackling a wide range of topics, data sets, and techniques. This type of portfolio is an excellent way for hiring managers to assess analysts' data visualization skills.

Dozens of people have used their #MakeoverMonday portfolio to find a new job. You will meet some of them later in this chapter.

3. Learn and Inspire

#MakeoverMonday gives participants and those just following the project a hefty dose of inspiration and the opportunity to learn something new every day. Aside from building technical skills, #MakeoverMonday, with its constant stream of data visualizations, shows participants and followers how a single data set can be visualized in dozens if not hundreds of different ways. Every week.

Many of our community members use this as an opportunity to learn about new approaches to communicating data and finding different ways to design a visualization or structure their storytelling.

"I am very grateful for participating and learning from this awesome project."

—*Sergiu Rotaru,*
https://twitter.com/SergiuRotaru6/status/1212842857486266368

"I recently started learning #R, so great to practice—that is what I love about MM, inspiration for learning."

—*Mateusz Karmalski,*
https://twitter.com/Mati_Karmalski/status/1207933287383142402

"Every week learning something new with #MakeoverMonday Today was slope graph."

—Emily Cebrat,
https://twitter.com/EmilyCebrat/status/1196732559058767875

Every person has the power to inspire others with their visualizations, by demonstrating their progress of learning, and by developing their own unique style. The inspiration people have found from #MakeoverMonday has extended into organizations as participants have taken their ideas and solutions back to their day jobs and shown others what can be done.

We have heard many times that people truly enjoy seeing every person take a different approach to the data set. Even if 10 people create a simple bar chart, each chart will be slightly different. That's the power of bringing people together in a community; everyone contributes in their own unique way, and the result is greater than what a single person could have created.

4. Grow Your Network

By now you understand how #MakeoverMonday brings people together. This happens virtually for the most part, but the exchanges people engage in help form real-life connections and relationships. We see this particularly when we hold live events, and community members who previously knew each other only through online interactions on Twitter suddenly are in the same room and able to connect in person.

For the most part, participants use their #MakeoverMonday network to learn from one another, to ask questions, to seek and provide feedback, and to congratulate each other on work well done.

As many of these connections are with people who also work in analytics, data science, and data visualization, many community members have used #MakeoverMonday to grow their professional network, to find talented people, to showcase their own skills to potential employers, and to connect with like-minded individuals.

We have witnessed dozens of participants take the next steps in their careers by participating in #MakeoverMonday. Many others have used their new skills and ideas to establish themselves as internal champions in their organizations. They have built communities of their own, sharing their knowledge and technical expertise, and helping others improve and develop much like they did.

5. Have an Impact

Choosing a different data set and topic each week for #MakeoverMonday eventually led us to finding opportunities to work with nonprofit organizations on social impact issues that needed highlighting. We have run a number of collaborations with nonprofits such as Operation Fistula, PATH's Visualize No Malaria, and the UN SDG Action Campaign, to give their data a bigger platform and to crowdsource visualizations and new ideas for storytelling from our community.

Our participants have always enjoyed data visualization challenges that gave them a chance to have a real impact on issues from gender equality, maternal health, and malaria prevention to the actions and changes committed to by individuals, organizations, and entire nations.

Connect to DEI. Values that matter to the community

Connecting data analysts and data visualization experts with nonprofits that often have very small capacity for analysis makes a big difference to these organizations and has an immediate impact on how widely and effectively they can share their message.

People of the #MakeoverMonday Community

The #MakeoverMonday community attracts people across the globe, including data professionals looking for a fun challenge or analysts at the start of their career, keen to build their skills and professional network. The people we discuss next have very different backgrounds, live in different parts of the world, and are at different points in their careers. They have used #MakeoverMonday for their personal and professional development.

community serves folks at all levels of career.

The first person I want to introduce you to is Meera Umasankar.

Meera Umasankar

Meera Umasankar, an assistant vice president at a leading international retail bank in Singapore, began her Makeover Monday journey because of her mentor, Sarah Burnett. Meera was inspired by Sarah's commitment to complete every #MakeoverMonday challenge in 2018. Looking for a new challenge to improve her data visualization skills, Meera began #MakeoverMonday in 2019 and completed all 53 challenges, earning several "Viz of the Day" recognitions from Tableau Public. Her work also was mentioned by us many times in our weekly "Favorites" blog.

In her own words, here are the key things Meera learned through her participation:

- The data sets are diverse
  #MakeoverMonday is all about visualizing various topics each week. While I was not familiar with all the topics, it was fascinating to take a deep dive into the data, analyze, and learn more.
- Approaching complex data sets
  I get carried away easily when there is a lot of information in a data set. One of the important things that I learned is that you don't have to visualize everything you see in the data set. Identify some of the key findings and build your own story.
- Visual best practices
  We read a lot about the best practices to be followed for designing a data visualization, and it is essential to incorporate and implement them in your weekly visualizations.
- Webinar feedback
  The weekly Viz Review webinars helped me develop my very own visualization style and design. After either receiving feedback on my own work or listening to the feedback given to others, I submit my updated visualization. Hearing the comments on everyone's work really helps me learn.
- Being creative
  In our day jobs, we do not always have the opportunity to be flexible or creative when it comes to data visualization. This project gave me a weekly opportunity to be innovative and to try out my own ideas.
- Connecting with people
  #MakeoverMonday allowed me to share my knowledge and passion for data visualization with people all around the world. I am an introvert, and this collaborative environment has boosted my confidence and connected me to some of the best talent in the Tableau community.

Meera made the weekly commitment to her own learning and development. Finding time for regular practice can be challenging, and here is Meera's approach:
- Make your weekly practice part of your routine.
- Prioritize tasks accordingly.

- Time box yourself to ensure you don't get carried away for too long.
- Dedicate a set amount of time to your practice.

Meera experienced a number of benefits from her consistent participation and has taken those lessons learned into her day job:

- Faster turnaround times
- Participating regularly in #MakeoverMonday influenced all her day-to-day actions and pursuits. It helped her minimize her turnaround time for data projects at work.

Meera was also inspired by her participation and that of others. Watching people come up with a diverse range of designs and approaches for the same data set each week has changed how she looks at and works with data. Now Meera pays more attention to every design detail, and her way of analyzing the data improved significantly.

She came to recognize the importance of developing your own style. Meera developed her own style of designing data visualizations and dashboards, a skill that she brings into her job and which results in more consistency in her work output.

On top of taking new skills and knowledge back to her job, Meera's career also benefited from her participation in Makeover Monday, mainly because it opened doors to bigger opportunities and instilled in her a newfound level of discipline. Her engagement with the community resulted in Meera being approached by the HR department of her previous employer through social media after they reviewed her portfolio. The interview focused on questions around her processes and approach to creating best practice visualizations, and Meera was offered the job instantly. Participating in #MakeoverMonday helped her build a strong and noticeable data visualization portfolio.

Source: Meera Umasankar

Another person I want to introduce you to is Zunaira Rasheed. She and I talked about her journey into data and data visualization.

Zunaira Rasheed

Author: Zunaira, how did you hear about #MakeoverMonday, and why did you decide to start participating?

Zunaira: I came across #MakeoverMonday purely by chance. Part of my job at the time was to perform exploratory analysis and present it to the management. While it was always well received, I was simply using Microsoft Excel and PowerPoint at that time and did not know much about data visualization except for how to make charts in Excel. I am always working to grow my skills because I believe there is always room for improvement and one should strive to be a better version of oneself in every aspect of life. So I wanted to learn about data visualization and I also wanted to know what other tools are out there. At that time, I had heard about Tableau and Power BI, but did not know much about either of them. I went online to look for more information and went from one search result to the next before ending up on Andy Kriebel's blog, where I discovered #MakeoverMonday.

It did not take long for me to realize that this was a community coming together to teach each other and learn from one another. I was thoroughly motivated to get involved.

Author: Did you join any of the weekly Viz Review webinars, and, if so, what did you think of that way of providing feedback?

Zunaira: At the time when I discovered #MakeoverMonday, I had not read about data visualization or taken any courses, so Viz Review was my first exposure to the dos and don'ts of visualization. Looking back, I think it was probably the best way to start my journey because what better way is there to learn than to create something and iterate based on feedback? The format of the feedback during Viz Review is most conducive to learning. It starts with looking at what works, what doesn't work, includes the reasons why something doesn't work and how to change a visualization so it communicates its message more effectively. I made it a habit to watch the weekly webinar even during weeks when I did not submit my own content. You can learn a lot simply by listening to feedback on other people's work, because there are always tips and tricks you can take away and implement in your own analysis.

By watching the webinar every week, I was able to develop a mental checklist, which helps me create better visualizations now using best practices.

Author: #MakeoverMonday helped you find a new job. How did this happen, and what do you think were the major factors that helped you succeed?

Zunaira: #MakeoverMonday was a big help when I started learning Tableau because there was data available to work on every single week. I participated whenever I could and gradually built my portfolio of visualizations without any particular goal in mind other than learning a new tool and data visualization concepts. One of my #MakeoverMonday visualizations was chosen as "Viz of the Day" by Tableau. This visualization caught the attention of my current employer, who saw the portfolio I had built through #MakeoverMonday and reached out to me. I was able to score the job, marking a major milestone in my career. Tableau and data visualization went from being a side passion project to being my day job.

Author: What advice would you give to people who want to get involved with data and analytics initiatives or communities but don't know where to start?

Zunaira: Communities like #MakeoverMonday, the wider data visualization community, and the Tableau community have some of the most supportive and understanding people. They make a conscious effort to welcome new participants and support them in getting started. I also suggest reaching out to like-minded people and to not be afraid to ask for help.
My decision to get involved in these communities has allowed me to grow and learn and presented opportunities that completely changed my life.

Source: Zunaira Rasheed

Meera and Zunaira are two dedicated members of our #MakeoverMonday community who joined the project without specific expectations and used it to fundamentally change their careers and their lives.

Whether your community is or will be a large one with hundreds of members or a smaller group of people, there are a number of lessons you can learn from the #MakeoverMonday people and from individuals like Meera and Zunaira.

Lessons from the #MakeoverMonday Community

Key lessons from #MakeoverMonday that you can use to grow or create a strong analytics community in your organization are discussed next.

Bringing People Together

At its core, building a community is about bringing people together for a common purpose and a shared passion or interest. What we experienced through #MakeoverMonday is that "build it and they will come" certainly has a lot of truth to it. When you create something that is easy to access and genuinely helps people, they will flock to it. Being able to connect people virtually or in person gives them the chance to meet a like-minded community and to see their work/interest from a different perspective. Seeing what community members are able to create and the ideas they come up with when they have the opportunity of deeper exchanges with others often yields surprising results and impressive outcomes.

Samo Drole, a product designer in the #MakeoverMonday community and someone who generously shares his tips, advice, and knowledge with others, was able to grow his professional network through his weekly participation. At first, he just wanted to practice and never thought of a network. But after producing and sharing more of his work, his network started to grow organically. People started to follow Samo and recognize his work. Over time he was able to meet a few people from this community in person and many more through social networks. He told me that he is very grateful that the shared passion for data visualization and #MakeoverMonday has brought people together.

Sharing Knowledge

In the #MakeoverMonday community, people thrive on the idea and process of sharing knowledge with others while gaining new skills and knowledge for themselves. When people see tangible benefits for their personal and professional development, they have a genuine incentive to become involved and stay engaged.

New participants in #MakeoverMonday may watch from the sidelines for a few weeks before tentatively publishing their first visualizations. Once they get started with the weekly challenges, they quickly realize the benefits that come from asking for feedback and interacting with others.

[handwritten margin note: Providing and receiving]

[handwritten margin note: Space for new folks to watch on sidelines as long as they want.]

For knowledge workers—and these are typically the types of people we see getting involved in #MakeoverMonday—a community that fosters their development of technical and soft skills is a valuable one to get involved with.

Creating a Platform for Sharing

We experimented with the way we would interact with our community, the technology used for sharing datasets, and the platform we use for the daily exchanges between participants. My biggest recommendation for choosing a platform is that it needs to be easy to access and to use, ideally free of charge, and it should foster collaboration. For #MakeoverMonday, we settled on Twitter for collaboration, data.world for sharing data, and our website (www.makeovermonday.co.uk) for easy access to all resources needed to participate, the blog for lessons learned, a gallery of favorite visualizations, webinar and workshop information, and quick access to our book.

could be multiple platforms

Establishing Sustainable and Scalable Processes

Starting a community is fun and exciting. The real work is in maintaining momentum and growing the community once the initial excitement wears off and the community operates in a business-as-usual mode. For people leading these analytics communities, it helps to create processes and structures that can be automated, take away some of the busywork, and allow for growth and potential changes in direction.

Here is a short overview of the processes that have made #MakeoverMonday successful:

- **Divide and conquer:** Split up the tasks so that each person finds 26 data sets for the year and is responsible for publishing information and creating the favorites for their respective weeks.
- **Collaboration tools:** We use a combination of Quip, Google Docs, Google Sheets, and Google Slides for collaboration. This helps us work from wherever we are, keep track of changes easily, and invite others to collaborate where necessary.
- **Ongoing communication:** Effective and deliberate communication between the project leaders helps to keep each other in the loop, offer help, share ideas, and identify when community members can use more guidance and support.

running the Community

- **Consistent schedule:** We have a very consistent, nonnegotiable schedule for the project as a whole, which makes things simpler and easier to automate. It also helps new members join the community more quickly. The weekly challenges are like merry-go-rounds that you can watch for as many rounds as you like before jumping on for the ride.

Empowering Others in Their Careers

#MakeoverMonday has helped us do something we didn't expect or predict: We helped dozens of people change the trajectory of their jobs and careers, sometimes even their lives. While we thought we were just publishing data, giving feedback, and sharing our favorite visualizations each week, many participants took their regular #MakeoverMonday practice and instilled new habits into their day jobs as well.

Countless people have built portfolios to showcase their analytical, design, and visualization skills, which helped them find new jobs or get promoted into their dream jobs.

Many of our participants want to do more work with data and want to work in jobs where analysis and visualization is the focus and takes up most of their time. #MakeoverMonday enabled them to build a network to find those jobs.

Ash Shih came out of nowhere in 2019 and dedicated his time to practicing, learning new skills, and improving the way he used data and visualization to tell compelling stories. He told me the #MakeoverMonday project had a large impact on him that year. Coming into #MakeoverMonday with minimal experience, the project gave him opportunities to practice and a framework to grow.

Ash was encouraged whenever his work was featured on the weekly #MakeoverMonday blog, as it helped him see the progress he was making in building his data visualization skills. As a result of creating a portfolio of his work, he landed a job focused on data visualization just a few months after he started participating in #MakeoverMonday. Ash now works at Illumina, a company that creates instruments for DNA sequencing, and he loves his job.

Chapter 3

Building a Data Visualization Community at the USAA

In the following chapters you will read and understand how to build a community in your organization. Before we get to that point, I want you to meet the team at USAA (United Services Automobile Association) who, at the time of writing, were at the beginning of their community journey, establishing their internal setup, and launching activities to bring like-minded people together.

Their catalyst had been the Tableau Conference, which several of their people attended. These people shared a passion for data visualization and returned home with a dream to keep that passion alive. Their first step to building their own internal data visualization community was to find champions representing various departments across USAA and to work on defining the mission that would guide their activities and initiatives.

define a mission

Identifying what they wanted to accomplish and contrasting it with what they could realistically accomplish was part of the process. While the initial activities took around three months, it was time well spent, investing in the right foundations for the work to come.

3 months to build community space

Elizabeth Harwood and Sarah Coyle from USAA's Data Visualization User Group (DVUG), as their community is called, shared their story with me so that it can serve the readers of this book in supporting future analysts in their communities.

When I asked them about the key factors that helped them successfully grow their community early on, Elizabeth and Sarah told me that embracing diversity was and is very important for them. They sought to have representation across the enterprise. Having passionate people champion the community was also critical for getting started. These people got involved because they believed in the mission and saw the opportunity for future members as well as the organization as a whole.

How will Sara Jenn and Katie participate?

The DVUG mission is to build "One data visualization community to share knowledge, processes, and best practices throughout the enterprise."

Elizabeth and Sarah attribute the tool-agnostic mission to part of the success. The community attracts people who want to learn, improve, and grow their skills, regardless of the software, frameworks, and methodologies they use in their day-to-day work.

When it comes to training and development, the DVUG takes a holistic view and recognizes that their diverse community requires a variety of training avenues ranging from formal training to self-paced training and data visualization challenges. They partner with their IT teams to ensure that when new tools and capabilities are rolled out across the enterprise, they have a strategic plan to ensure successful user adoption. By offering varied training formats (e.g., instructor led, virtual, hands-on, office hours, etc.) and recording all sessions, the DVUG enable their geographically dispersed community to interact on a schedule that works best for them. Additionally, they believe training transcends tools and should encompass human-centered design, storytelling, and best practices.

At this early stage in their development, the team around Elizabeth and Sarah has received very positive feedback from members of their community and is planning a survey to assess the impact of the DVUG activities. Consistent growth of their community is a sign that things are heading in the right direction. With further maturity, the team plans to measure the increase in skill and data literacy.

In the long term, the DVUG goals are to:

1. Foster best practices.

2. Run regular challenges and competitions around data visualization.

3. Drive education.

4. Grow the community.

These four areas are the focus for the team in their first year. Eventually it would like to have fully dedicated team members running the community and a center of excellence at USAA.

The DVUG goals of education and fostering best practices are supported by an active and pragmatic approach to training. In some instances, formal technical training can be provided, but scaling this offering is not always feasible immediately, so the DVUG encourages internal champions and experts to share their knowledge via in-person and virtual training sessions. This approach results in various specializations emerging and niche topics being covered. Members are encouraged to utilize existing enterprise social channels to "join the conversation and share," to enable informal and ad hoc learning, and to enable the exchange between employees across the organization.

To bring different ideas and perspectives into the community, the DVUG team invites external speakers and experts to present to and engage with their people. USAA employees also engage with the wider data visualization community by attending local user groups. Elizabeth, Sarah, and their team are working on building a series of events with external speakers to ensure that their community can connect with experts in the field, get answers to their question, find new inspiration, and identify new learning opportunities. Those who get to attend these events will then share their experiences and lessons learned with the community at USAA.

When I asked Elizabeth and Sarah about their advice for organizations wanting to establish their own analytics and data focused communities, they stated how important it was for them to learn from their first attempt to build the DVUG. They picked apart what worked and what did not work and aimed to address those challenges the second time around. Maintaining a balance between ambitious goals and the realities of day-to-day business was one of their recommendations, as was finding representatives from across the enterprise to become part of the community.

PART II

Chapter Four

Benefits of Setting Up Communities

Everything that is worth doing typically requires a bit of effort. The same is true for creating, growing, and developing an analytics community in your organization. Yes, it will take some time to establish, and it will require commitment, resources, and people who take ownership and responsibility. The return will make it all worthwhile for the organization, its bottom line, and, importantly, the individuals involved and the person or team that brings everyone together.

In this chapter, we explore some of the benefits that organizations can achieve by setting up an analytics community. We look at the advantages that can be gained and measured and the outcomes that are intangible or more difficult to quantify, especially at a group and individual level.

Benefits for an Organization

Let's start by looking at the direct and indirect benefits an organization can achieve when establishing, fostering, and growing an internal analytics community.

Direct Benefits

Benefits that stand out for most organizations concern efficiencies and productivity gains. These can be achieved by analytics communities, first and foremost, through improved communication and transparency.

Connecting analysts across the business and encouraging them to share what they are working on, the challenges they face, and the business questions they are tackling gives them the chance to discover gaps and overlaps. Often people work on similar problems without knowing it; once they are connected, they can work together to overcome the challenges. Collaborations make way for genuine improvements of processes and outputs and help people have measurable impact.

what people are coming together to share [handwritten margin note]

Return on Investment

What about the investment organizations make in analytics overall and the people, tools, and processes in particular? I argue that an analytics community allows leaders to prove and increase the return on investment. How do these communities achieve that?

First, analytics communities bring people together, showing the size and extent of analytics in the organization and creating a loose network of people who have similar and complementary skills, use similar techniques and tools to do their work, and access the same or similar systems. Often people work on questions and analyses that, at the fundamental level, are similar, using data and information to obtain answers to questions and provide decision-making support.

Second, analytics communities tend to improve and increase the use of available tools. As people connect with one another and start collaborating, exchanging ideas and helping each other, they will make visible their own expertise, methodologies, and development requirements. This in turn will lead to people learning more and more from one another, learning more about the tools they use, and growing their own skills, especially technical skills.

As a result, processes, solutions, guidelines, and approaches will be developed that allow people, especially less experienced analysts, to gain skills and become competent faster.

Many organizations that have thriving analytics communities report a strong level of adoption and use of analytics tools and software. Having an engaged analytics community in your organization will strengthen your existing user base for available software while also increasing adoption with new users as they can access a larger amount of resources.

Third, analytics communities can help identify the need for change and improvement to existing tools, systems, and processes. A single analyst may discover an issue and be able to address it, but unearthing problems is more likely using the collective intelligence of a community as well as the increased exposure to issues that comes from having many people work on different questions and business areas. Identifying those problems, making them visible, and addressing them is important when it comes to the ROI of analytics in an organization because issues that are not addressed can become expensive and difficult to deal with farther down the track.

Fourth, again with the collective power of smart people using data and the right tools to find answers for an organization, businesses can ensure that their investment in analytics pays for itself. Setting specific targets for and measuring the impact of analysts helps make the impact visible.

Training and Development

Organizations with established analytics communities report their benefit in providing continuous training and development to their staff. Those in the process of setting up such communities are aiming for internal training programs to become an integral part of the company.

Fundamentally, more experienced people teach those around them, and the entire community experiences an increase in skills and expertise. This training often focuses on the technical aspects of an analyst's job, and rightly so. Such aspects include:

- Statistical analysis concepts
- Software skills
- Effective communication of information
- Storytelling
- Data visualization, including the use of colors, layout, and design

All of these are important skills to learn and should be complemented by soft skills that are essential for any successful analyst to have. These soft skills include:

- Stakeholder management
- Requirements analysis
- Listening
- Communication
- Business acumen
- Managing relationships across the business
- A willingness to share knowledge and information with others
- Fostering an inclusive culture of continuous professional development
- Advocating for the use of data in decision-making processes

In short, analysts should not limit themselves to creating and sharing information. They should also consider their potential influence in the organization to make analytics a core process for decision making and strategy.

Analytics communities must foster professional training and development and ensure that people keep their skill levels current in a market that moves at a fast pace and pushes organizations to pursue data as an asset for competitive advantage.

At the very minimum, once community members are connected to each other, they can start asking and **answering each other's questions**. Ideally, they use a platform or collaboration tool, such as Slack, Yammer, Chatter, or similar, to post their questions, get their answers, have discussions, and make the content visible for others. Many software vendors, for example, have discussion forums with extensive search features so users can find available content quickly.

A number of large organizations have implemented their own resources internally to structure access to content in a very transparent and user friendly way. One example comes from a large UK bank that has successfully implemented a knowledge exchange where people can find answers to their questions. In the past, teams used to be very siloed and found it difficult to communicate and to share data. Now, with the new platform in place, sharing and communication have improved significantly. Analysts, data scientists, and business-people can access resources they did not even know existed because they are now connected through digital channels across the entire organization.

Communication Tool

It all started with one department, which was an early adopter of Tableau Software for analytics. At the start, people found it difficult to operate the solution within the existing framework. Dealing with the various pain points, members of the department decided they wanted to reduce barriers for other teams that would implement Tableau into their work, so they started documenting all their pain points and solutions using a knowledge management tool called Hive. People started answering each other's questions and started publishing blog articles with ideas and solutions.

As the bank has stringent security settings, analysts found it difficult to access public resources, such as community pages, which meant they had to build their own content. Through their knowledge exchange they created a safe space to share, learn, and ask questions. The platform gained momentum because people received recognition for their contributions. This in turn helped them become recognized as data experts and created opportunities for them in their career across the organization.

The knowledge exchange was started by the team using Tableau, but within the bank multiple tools exist. Pippa Law, who manages the community, confirmed that they are now starting to see the different communities coming together around different software and tackling technical challenges and questions, such as how to integrate the solutions of separate departments with their enterprise-wide big data lake. The ultimate goal for her community is to merge and integrate tools, processes, and teams across the business.

If we consider the process of answering each other's questions as the first step, then **creating lasting content** is certainly the second step. The collective of the communities can form valuable content over time, structuring resources, tagging and cataloging them digitally so that anyone searching for help can find answers quickly and effectively.

Whether content is hosted on a shared drive or in a cloud environment, the focus should be on the user experience. Certainly quality of the content is essential, but if users cannot find or access it, even the best-quality materials are useless. Documentation, articles, templates, examples, scripts, and reusable content should be easy to access and as openly available to community members as possible. The better this access, the easier it is for everyone to use and learn from the content.

For the organization, this results in a community that can help itself and analysts who can take responsibility for their own learning and skill development.

It is critical for knowledge workers to stay up-to-date with their skills and expertise, continuously developing their professional skill set to keep it relevant to the demands of the organizations they are working in. Many organizations, especially larger corporations, have **developed formal internal training and development programs** and send their people on external training, such as leadership or technical courses.

It is not uncommon, however, for training and development opportunities to be given as incentives for high performers rather than being accessible to the wider staff population. In some businesses, access to training is nonexistent, because of an expectation that people come equipped with the necessary skills and expertise. Some organizations are afraid that if they train their employees, they will leave. But what if they do not go through the training and they stay?

In the world of data analytics, new developments regarding software and systems happen at a rapid pace, and the influence of data science and data engineering put pressure on people to upskill continuously. Analytics communities are an excellent environment to offer the much-needed training opportunities for anyone working with data. One of the many benefits is that this training can be provided in a cost effective way.

Next I outline a few informal and formal approaches to training.

Informal Training Sessions

Informal sessions are a great way to engage people who are new to working with data, who might be new to the organization, or who cannot currently commit to the demands of a more formal training program.

Casual Meetups

Community leaders and champions, as well as those with more experience, can offer their time to sit down with colleagues and help them address a technical or analytical problem. The ad hoc meetings are likely to already happen on occasion, but it helps to develop a way to make them more visible and accessible.

In my own work environment, for example, I regularly remind colleagues to seek out my input on specific topics and to ask for help in my area of expertise. I also set up spontaneous presentations (in person or via video conference) to explain certain aspects around data visualization and Tableau, demonstrating how something works or why things are done a certain way. What drives these interactions are typically specific questions, challenges, or discussions. Taking 10 to 15 minutes to show people how something works instead of simply explaining it has made a big difference. For me personally, these sessions are great ways to continuously challenge myself to find clear and simple explanations for potentially complex technical or analytical concepts.

Lunch & Learn Sessions

I am the first to encourage people to step away from their desks during their breaks, but I am also a fan of occasional lunch & learn sessions where someone runs a presentation and hosts a subsequent discussion, and people get to share food at the same time.

I participated in these kinds of sessions early on in my career, where my peers and I would learn about customer use cases or build our industry knowledge during a shared lunch. I have also presented to colleagues as well as customers and partners in these kinds of settings. The benefits are that the lunch setting makes for a relaxed environment, one where participants are more likely to debate and discuss. It's like an engaging dinner party with friends.

While I hesitate to recommend a deep technical how-to session while people eat sushi and sandwiches, having lunch & learn sessions to share information, bring in external speakers, and bring together people from different parts of the organization is definitely a worthwhile exercise.

Walk-bys

Sometimes the best conversations and aha moments happen when someone walks by their colleague's desk, strikes up a conversation, and is able to solve a problem on the fly. Even within an office, many people these days communicate through messenger apps. Communicating face-to-face is invaluable. I have learned a lot from colleagues who came to discuss one topic and ended up showing me something, helping me figure out an analytical or data problem, and left me with new knowledge and fresh ideas.

I encourage you to use face-to-face interactions where possible to create these learning opportunities and to strengthen interpersonal relationships within your organization.

Call for Help

We cannot leave our training and that of our colleagues up to chance encounters, as enjoyable as those may be. Sometimes we simply need to ask for help, especially when dealing with a specific problem or question. Ideally, people who need assistance already know whom to ask and can contact them directly. If not, then they need a platform or system where they can get the necessary support.

A ticketing system for IT queries is one option, but an analytics community also benefits from a less formal and more interactive approach, such as a help channel in a messaging app. For people to find answers to their questions, it is helpful to have access to many experts at the same time. For the experts, these calls for help have the potential to be disruptive to the task they are working on, so having a shared platform ensures that enough people are available to answer questions and the expectation is set at the right level—that is, not everyone needs to drop everything to answer a question and there is enough expertise to help out.

Structured and Formal Training Sessions

To embed the principles of continuous professional development and the importance of learning into the culture of the organization, it is important to formalize training at a level that is appropriate for the size and structure of the analytics community.

Establishing Regular Sessions

The simplest way to add more structure to your existing setup is to schedule regular sessions and to publish this schedule so people can participate and commit to frequent practice.

For #MakeoverMonday, our schedule is weekly with data being published every Sunday and with Monday and Tuesday being the main days for engagement. Keeping the same rhythm throughout the project:

- Makes the project easier to manage, as the same type of work happens on the same day each week.
- Allows us to automate tasks as much as possible.
- Brings transparency and predictability for members, especially those participating for the first time.
- Makes it easy for people to enter the project, as there is certainty about its structure.
- Allows us to build a brand with elements such as webinars and regular blog posts that deliver value to our community and visibility across media channels.

Building a brand

While our project runs on a weekly cadence, it is fine to have less frequent interactions. There could be, for example, a monthly lunch & learn session with the responsibility of presenting being rotated from one member to the next. Or a biweekly internal webinar could offer specific features or highlight use cases for analytics software.

Finding the right number of sessions might require a bit of testing; what's most important is consistency. Start with a monthly cadence to test adoption and to create a curriculum for the 12 months ahead. Seek out volunteers for presentations and training sessions. A few months into it, you will know whether this frequency works. If there is a stronger-than-expected demand, you can add further sessions and events to the schedule. If attendance is on the low side, consider moving the formal sessions to a quarterly schedule and leave some space for ad hoc events and presentations if demand increases.

figure out frequency

External Experts and Trainers

An engaging and motivating way to train your people is to bring in external experts to speak about a certain topic or facilitate a workshop or training session. Industry experts can provide stimulating input for your people, especially when there is discussion afterward and an opportunity to connect. For some teams or organizations, however, this option may not be affordable, so consider alternatives as well.

The communities I am part of have many members with interesting stories to share, specialist skills, or experience. External speakers do not have to be world-renowned experts; they just need to inject something fresh and interesting. Check your network for connections you already have.

A number of people I am connected to regularly go into organizations to present on a topic of their expertise. This external input can bring a big boost to a community. Seeing and hearing a fresh perspective can take people out of their ruts and encourage them to try new and different approaches to their work.

Similarly, external trainers can become a valuable asset for your analytics community. They can validate what has already been done and can take your staff's skills to the next level in the course of a few hours or a couple of days. Investing in these external sources of knowledge, expertise, and experience also shows those being trained that they are valued and that efforts are being made to continuously expand their skill set.

Train the Trainer

After some time and the introduction of formalized training, you may discover that the community has grown to a certain size—a size that warrants further structuring of the training you offer. To do this and to maintain cost effectiveness, consider sending one or two of your strongest community members on a train the trainer session so they can formalize their expertise and pass on their knowledge internally. Doing this means that instead of relying on external trainers, you can draw on your internal champions who can teach technical and business skills and do so within the context of your organizational culture.

The benefits of doing this are not limited to having official trainers internally who can teach certain processes or the use of certain software. These champions are now better at teaching others more generally, having learned about adult education, about presenting and demonstrating content, and about engaging with a classroom full of colleagues. Building this kind of mindset and expertise helps you further build a sharing culture within your analytics community.

Internal Events

Once your community has gained momentum and the internal training, both informal and formal, is running smoothly, likely there will come a point when someone will suggest an internal event. So far you may have done presentations, webinars, and training sessions, but they probably were standalone items on your community agenda.

You now have the opportunity to combine the existing elements into an event, half a day or even a whole day, stringing together presentations, hands-on sessions, and discussions. Here are a few ideas to consider, with more details on how to run these events in later parts of the book.

- An internal hackathon, where different teams or individuals work on solving a specific question or challenge. You could use a specific data set and ask people for insights. Bringing everyone together, even those who are new to the subject, can result in great outcomes, new ideas and approaches, while requiring minimal cost or risk.

- A showcase event where different teams present some of their work during a morning session, bookended by networking over coffee and cake or lunch. This brings together different teams across the business and might uncover opportunities for collaboration.

- A technical mini-conference that includes a talk about the value of data to the organization, followed by presentations from internal speakers and a hands-on training session.

- An internal user group that combines the elements of the mini-conference with the focus on a specific software. Talks could feature use cases, example outputs (applications, dashboards, reports, etc.), technical tips, and recent success stories.

- A panel discussion, featuring experts and leaders from across the organization, sharing their views on analytics and the role it plays for the success of the business. Providing access to these people via an open-mic round or Q&A at the end provides an opportunity for input from the community while also connecting their work with what drives leadership in their decision making.

Indirect Benefits

Aside from the quantifiable advantages that come with establishing and developing an analytics community, there are benefits that may not be so obvious at first. These positive outcomes tend to take a little more time to come about, and they are typically not the main reason why organizations establish these communities. Being able to go beyond the easily measurable and into qualitative outcomes gives people a way to make their impact visible.

Creating a Culture of Continuous Improvement

Analysts and data professionals deal with numbers on a daily basis. As they create outputs that serve as decision-making bases for leadership teams, the results must be reliable and accurate. Analysts cannot become complacent about their professional skills and need to seek input and feedback from others.

To create a culture of continuous improvement, you must first establish a feedback culture. This is an environment where feedback is encouraged, so people ask for feedback and provide it to others. It needs to be safe to do so. If people fear being penalized for going through an iterative process where their work is reviewed, they may not be open to suggestions and ideas from others, and improvement will be much harder to achieve.

Essentially, you need to make people feel comfortable when asking for others' input. It should be a normal process they go through when doing their job. People seeking feedback benefit by getting help to become better. Those providing feedback enjoy watching the receivers implement their suggestions and develop their skills.

There are a number of different ways to **establish a feedback culture in your analytics community**, but the key ingredient is transparency; it is critical to talk openly about the need for a working feedback process and how constructive critique helps people address their professional, technical, and soft skills development needs. You should make it very clear that the feedback people receive should be relevant and not personal attacks. The feedback must be about the content, not the person who created it.

Here are some ways of building a feedback culture:

- **One-on-one sessions:** Sitting down with a colleague and talking with them through their work can be a great way to ease into the feedback process. I always approach this step by asking people questions about their approach and about alternative methodologies and designs. This gives them the opportunity to arrive at the solution themselves and provides them with a question catalog they can use in the future when reviewing their own work.
- **Implement team sessions as appropriate:** I do not suggest picking people's work apart in front of their peers. Working with a team is an opportunity to get everyone around the table to share their input and critique. Laying ground rules is important here to ensure the tone stays professional and the outcome is constructive.

- **Find neutral ground:** For #MakeoverMonday, we find poorly designed visualizations from the internet and ask our community to create better visualizations of the same data. We also ask them to critically evaluate the original chart. Having a common base to work from that comes from outside our community means that everyone looks at the same visualization to start with and reflects on the positive and negative aspects before creating their own makeovers. Where possible, use these situations to further show how important it is to critically evaluate the information in front of users.

have something from outside to iterate on.

After some time you will likely notice people ask their peers for feedback without being prompted. Whether colleagues offer themselves as an audience to someone practicing their next presentation or sit in a room to review an analyst's findings, this is the kind of culture you want to build. It will allow you to move to the next phase, where people are comfortable with taking apart the work they previously created, work they were probably very proud of when they completed it and now realize it would benefit from improvements.

Organizations that strive to have highly skilled and well-trained people will attract like-minded people with talents that can lead to a competitive advantage and have a lasting impact on the success of the business. Successful, data-driven businesses **encourage strong technical and interpersonal skills.** Making continuous improvement a pillar of your culture means building an environment where high performers can thrive and where people want to work.

Over the years, I have met many people in the analytics industry who have a hunger for knowledge and who are not content with coasting along in a comfortable job. They are highly skilled and want to use these skills to make a difference, to help their organization perform, to achieve its mission, and to feel a personal sense of satisfaction. Smart knowledge workers know that their expertise and their ability to learn and adapt is their most valuable asset, so supporting these people and encouraging their job satisfaction will pay dividends for your organization.

Uplifting everyone's skills is always a worthwhile investment.

Appealing to Future Talent

Becoming known for building a culture of continuous professional development is great for the staff you already have. It also attracts other talented people to join your organization and your analytics community. The expectations of such a culture are not just about the organization providing training opportunities but also about each employee showing an interest in and making an effort to build their skills, grow their knowledge, and develop relevant valuable experiences that help achieve the organization's strategy over the long term.

Attracting like-minded people who will rise to that challenge and bring their unique talents, ideas, and problem-solving skills is an advantage for your business, especially in a time where it can be difficult to find and secure those people for open roles. What attracts data professionals to an organization?

- Seeing a clear development path within the analytics department and the wider organization
- Understanding how their contributions can make a difference and have an impact on achieving the overall organizational goals and targets
- Seeing how they can become part of the analytics community and share their expertise with their peers
- Having access to industry experts and the right tools to do their work effectively and produce the right outputs and outcomes
- Working with like-minded professionals with the options to collaborate on projects, data challenges, and to solve business questions

Industry Leadership

Some organizations embrace their data as a valuable asset. Then there are those that do not. There is not much in between. Traditional businesses aiming to be or become data-driven are all progressing at different paces toward this goal. If we set aside data-rich tech companies, such as Google, Facebook, and Amazon, and look at banking, insurance, automotive, pharmaceuticals, and retail industries, we can see that there are many businesses that collect massive amounts of data from their customers, suppliers, factories, and employees.

Doing something meaningful with all these data is good for business and, in my view, also necessary. If the data are not being used, after all, why are they being collected in the first place?

This book presents a number of organizations that have established internal analytics communities that set them apart from their competitors. When analysts, data engineers, or data scientists have the choice between a few competing organizations, they likely will choose a place where they can thrive, bring their talents and skills into the business in a meaningful way, and see that analytics and data are considered essential to the organization's strategy and success. Your analytics community can certainly be a differentiator within your industry and make your organization appealing to future employees.

Benefits for the Analytics Industry

The existence, development, and continued growth of analytics communities are good things for the analytics industry as a whole. These communities help a lot of people from nontechnical backgrounds enter the world of data. People from across an organization are recognizing the need to become data literate and to work with data as part of their day jobs. Becoming part of the company's internal analytics community gives them access to the people and resources that can help them acquire the necessary knowledge and skills to analyze data and communicate insights and information effectively.

How do we make sure we're not talking over people's heads? How will Zulema participate?

Growing Technical and Soft Skills

While universities teach statistics and have been offering more and more data analytics courses and degrees in recent years, they cannot do all the heavy lifting when it comes to skill building. Most data literacy, analytical, and communication skills are built on the job through projects, assignments, tasks, and regular feedback and input from others. Bringing together people internally to connect those with less experience and knowledge to employees who have a deep technical understanding of analytics and strong business knowledge helps to lift skills across the board.

Those new to data analytics learn valuable skills, techniques, and methodologies. The experienced people learn to teach and share their knowledge while also enhancing their own skills (because when you teach, you really need to know what you are talking about).

When analytics communities grow internally and across an industry, when they develop more formalized training approaches, talent also grows. As people naturally progress through their careers and move onto new opportunities, they contribute to spreading these skills further and injecting fresh ideas and knowledge into other parts of any organizations they join.

Faster Progress

When people work together on a shared goal, they are going to be faster than if an individual chips away at a task by themselves. Remember the old saying, "Many hands make light work."

Today's for-profit and not-for-profit organizations often involve people in different locations working on different things. However, in many situations, once people start discussing their work, they realize that they would do well to team up for a task or project. These situations typically have one of the following scenarios:

- An analyst is working on a specific business question, while another analyst somewhere else is trying to do almost exactly the same thing.
- Teams in different locations are keen to build their technical skills and are looking for expertise.
- An individual has a specific analytical or technical question and is trying to figure out the answer on their own and through online resources.
- A team wants to start using a certain software or system and is going through a cumbersome approval process, while a team in another location has already completed these steps.

There are plenty of other scenarios, but in essence, the problem is a lack of communication and transparency about what everyone is doing. I would argue, though, that most of the time these omissions are entirely unintentional. Also, it is not practical for every person and every team to report what they are working on just in case someone might find it useful. If instead an organization can set up ways for people and teams to ask for help and assistance, then the efforts of providing answers and solutions are more targeted and time can be used more effectively.

Analytics communities in organizations present ideas, methodologies, and outputs that are not just smart ways of using data and visualizations to communicate information. These assets help the industry move forward and do things differently and better. Bringing people together facilitates that shift. Organizations that strive to bring people together internally make a noticeable contribution to their industries.

Building a Global Network of Experts

With more and more organizations setting up and growing their analytics communities, globally we can witness a growing interconnectedness. Many companies and nonprofit organizations are dispersed and have people working across geographies, including remote work from home. Over time the conscious effort of connecting data professionals strengthens the overall network of people and gives remote workers an opportunity to find like-minded professionals nearby.

When you set up your community or as you build the one you already have, give your people the opportunity to join and participate from wherever they are. Small things, such as alternating the timing of webinar sessions or live events and their broadcasts to accommodate different time zones, make big differences for the people who are not located in a central location or headquarters.

Benefits for the Individual

I touched on some of the benefits for individuals as members of an analytics community earlier, and it warrants a deeper discussion. Through my own experience of being part of such communities and through my leading of #MakeoverMonday, I have seen firsthand what a difference being part of a community can make to an individual analyst, how it contributes to and facilitates their growth, and how it paves the path for their own contributions to the communities they are part of.

Learning and Development

First and foremost, these communities are excellent places for analysts to grow their skills. The pace of development of business intelligence and analytics tools is rapid, and keeping up with new features and capabilities requires a significant amount of self-guided learning. A lot of this learning can happen through observation, through active participation in regular activities, and through consistent feedback processes. Formal training cannot realistically cover all of this learning at scale and within budget.

With #MakeoverMonday, we have seen individuals participate diligently week in, week out and reap the rewards. Many of them have made great improvements in the ways they analyze and visualize data and communicate information and share their insights. When we compare their first submissions with later ones, what stands out is how much more clearly and effectively they communicate data and information and how their skills have grown over time.

Certain structures need to be in place so people can succeed, gain new knowledge, and develop their skills. Often simply being an active member of an analytics community will be a motivating factor.

Access to Experts

Individuals benefit from having direct access to the experts around them. Not just for learning technical skills, but also coaching and mentoring them in their career journey. People who strive to excel in data analytics and want to shape their careers in this field can gain from being connected to those with more experience who are willing and able to coach and guide them and who champion their cause.

Experience Job Enrichment and Satisfaction

Doing your job can be satisfying on its own, and for that reason, many people enjoy challenges that require their skills and expertise. Today's working world is markedly different from the work environments we found ourselves in 10 or 20 years ago. People are much more connected, while companies also operate on a much more global scale. New challenges have arisen to have flexible and mobile workers who are smart and capable while also being loyal to their employers.

Add to this the influx into the job market of a new digital native generation, with young workers who are tech savvy and ambitious and want their work to have an impact, ideally from day 1. With this new generation you will get a mix of views, mindsets, and approaches, and sometimes it is difficult to align everyone to a common vision or goal. Organizations with an analytics community have the opportunity to bring everyone together, allowing people to learn from one another, regardless of their age and experience.

Your data professionals may focus on data science, solving analytical problems with languages such as R and Python, or maybe their task is to roll out a global standardized reporting solution, or perhaps they work on creating interactive data visualizations. These situations can get people excited about the task at hand and break away from their traditional roles and potential structural silos. Focusing on the problem that needs solving rather than where someone sits in the hierarchy levels the playing field. People can benefit from one another in an environment that encourages and incentivizes sharing and openness.

A number of people have confirmed to me that becoming part of a data community (whether internal or external) helped them learn, and subsequently they become much more satisfied in their jobs. They were able to do things they previously had no knowledge of and earned new responsibilities at work. They also reported that sharing their knowledge and new skills with their peers made them more confident and showed them the impact they could have in their organizations. As Mahfooj Khan, Visual Analytics Manager at Beinex, said, "Community is the only place where we learn and teach at the same time."

Building Something of Value for the Organization

The projects, outputs, and initiatives that come out of analytics communities are far greater than any individual can achieve on their own. By being part of a community, people in your organization can have a greater impact and create something that takes their individual contributions farther.

Some people might really enjoy teaching others and can collaborate to create an internal curriculum for teaching analysis and data visualization skills. This curriculum can be their legacy and is something the organization will benefit from long term, while it helps individuals to push themselves in building value.

Others may be part of the data engineering team, and their achievement will be to build an enterprise-ready data warehouse for all analytics tasks. Again, there is great benefit for the organization, and the individuals get the sense of achievement from completing their task and delivering value.

Together, your analysts, data engineers, and data scientists can drive changes and improvements that generate many ideas, projects, and initiatives to help your organization make the most of its data.

→ Communities Create something

Chapter Five

Why Are Communities Important?

Earlier I claimed that there are a number of benefits to building an analytics community in your organization. Why are these communities important now, and how is the nature of work changing to give rise to these communities and initiatives?

Because analytics, and data as an industry, is a relatively new field, there are bound to be developments, changes, and innovations. People and organizations are still finding their places and struggling to make sense of the flood of information. With globally operating organizations, knowledge work has become more mobile, detached from a specific location. Skilled workers themselves can move more easily to other cities, states, and countries.

As individuals, we carry our knowledge, experience, and skills with us, wherever we go, and this can give us confidence and reassurance when everything else changes around us. Arriving in a new place—whether in a new role, a new organization, or a new country—comes with many challenges, including the question: Where do I fit in?

Sophia Dembling writes in *Psychology Today* that "community helps fulfill our very human need for connection without actually requiring a lot from us."[1]

In our professional lives, we often strive for success in a rather solitary pursuit. Yes, we work in teams and see our colleagues every day, but often the responsibility for and ownership of a successful outcome of a task is with the individual. Add to that the high demand for data and analytics professionals in the employment market. This means companies are competing for the best talent, and that talent is very much attached to each individual person.

What Communities Give to the Individual

In describing the importance of analytics communities in today's organizations, I want to highlight the very human aspects of connection and belonging that play a significant role in making us feel part of something bigger than ourselves.

The human brain is hard-wired for social connections, according to Matthew Lieberman, author of *Social: Why Our Brains Are Wired to Connect*. Over millions of years of evolution, our need for and desire to connect with others has emerged as an essential factor for survival, for thriving and succeeding.[2] In a community, we become part of a group that focuses on a shared interest, goal, or understanding.

Being excluded from a group can be painful and upset us. In a work context, exclusion certainly can impact our performance. Your analytics community will bring people together and will address their need for social interactions in the work environment, opening up opportunities to connect, cooperate, and collaborate.

In the #MakeoverMonday community, new members in particular are surprised by the supportive and encouraging camaraderie that exists in this virtual social project that brings people together around a shared passion for data analysis. Those who work in smaller teams or organizations or who

---

[1]Sophia Dembling, "Why Even Introverts Need Community," *Psychology Today*, February 18, 2015, https://www.psychologytoday.com/us/blog/the-introverts-corner/201502/why-even-introverts-need-community

[2]Matthew Lieberman, *Social: Why Our Brains Are Wired to Connect* (New York: Crown, 2013).

are located remotely, away from their core team, can use the virtual #Make-overMonday community as a place for connection, for forming professional friendships with like-minded people, and for getting help with their projects and analytical challenges.

As a project that is run free of charge, #MakeoverMonday hosts a diverse community of people and sees a constant influx of new members who are supported by existing, more experienced participants. These invisible and very real support structures bring a dynamic of reliability and transparency where everyone can find their place and become part of the larger group. Their individual contributions, focused on design, analytical approaches, technical details, advanced visualization techniques, or written data stories, enrich the community for everyone.

The analytics community you have established or are in the process of building will become a place people can gravitate to and want to be a part of. For this to happen, your community needs to be as open and welcoming as possible. You can certainly have criteria for what the community will focus on and who you would like to involve in projects. Remember, though, to remove any barriers to entry and to keep community activities and projects visible and transparent.

As an exercise, think of the communities you are and have been part of during your life so far. They can be sports clubs, religious institutions, local communities, or any other group of people you feel connected to.

- What is the purpose of the community, and why do people come together?
- What feelings do you associate with being part of this community?
- What are some of your favorite memories from the activities you were involved in?
- What personal growth have you noticed through being part of the community?
- Have the connections you made influenced your personal life?
- What are some of the opportunities in your personal and professional life that you can attribute to being an active member of this community?
- If you were to leave the community or group, what would you miss the most?

Writing down or simply thinking through the answers to these questions will clarify some of the impact you have experienced personally through being in a community.

When I asked Zunaira Rasheed some of these questions, this is what she said: "Communities like #makeovermonday . . . have some of the most supportive and understanding people. They make a conscious effort to welcome newbies and highlight their work. They lift each other up. . . . My decision to get involved in these communities has allowed me to grow, learn, and has presented opportunities that I did not have before."

I encourage more people in the business world to embrace the social and emotional well-being that comes with being part of a group. Doing so will drive positive outcomes for the individuals, the community, and the organization as a whole.

What Each of Us Brings to a Community

Every member of a community brings their own contributions beyond their skills and knowledge. As humans we are capable of empathy and of understanding others by imagining ourselves in their situation. We are able to anticipate and imagine other people's responses, which gives us an unparalleled capacity for cooperation and collaboration.[3]

How do we use these skills? How can we bring together our analytical thinking and our capacity for social thinking?

As knowledge workers, we are often tempted to define our skills in terms of technical expertise, measurable output, intellect, and our ability to quickly gain new knowledge and understand new concepts. Our brains, however, are wired to see the world socially and to interpret others' actions in terms of the minds behind them.[4]

To help your colleagues leverage the power of community to build their skills and knowledge, I recommend you take a social approach that includes having peers teach one another, as this has been shown to be a more effective way of learning than memorizing information. Focusing on more than technical skills and embracing the value of social skills acknowledges the human element of your community, no matter what work context it operates in.

---

[3]Matthew Lieberman, "The Social Brain and Its Superpowers," TEDx Talks, October 7, 2013, https://youtu.be/NNhk3owF7RQ?t=570
[4]Ibid.

Regardless of industry, location, and organization size, when people come together to solve analytical challenges, find answers to business questions, and increase and improve the use of data-driven decision making, they are respected for the human factor they bring to their work.

If you can enable your people to feel truly connected with one another in the work environment, they will work to complement each others' strengths and weaknesses within the group, leading to better outcomes overall. Helping people grow their social skills makes those social skills a multiplier that lets you leverage the analytical skills of the wider group more effectively.

And for leaders like yourself? In addition to your ability to produce results, strong social skills are important factors in helping people respect you as a great leader.

How to Foster Constructive Connections in Your Analytics Community

When working with highly skilled, geographically dispersed, analytically minded, and curious people, how can you foster an environment where they want to participate?

This section details various activities you can set up to drive outputs, offer training, and upskill the community as a whole while showing the value your community adds to the wider organization.

What about the interpersonal relationships, the connections between people, and the potential for conflict?

I recommend focusing on four pillars based on my own experience in building and managing communities. These areas concern how we as people interact, communicate, and address any issues, and can be summarized as:

1. Feedback

2. Transparency

3. Listening

4. Regular reviews

Feedback

The best way for any of us to improve what we do is by seeking and receiving feedback. We learn from a very early age that others—parents, family, friends, teachers, or strangers—will give us feedback to help us learn something new. Asking for feedback and receiving it graciously is a difficult thing to do, and I applaud anyone who regularly listens to frank, constructive feedback in order to improve.

Acting on feedback is the important next step, so that the new knowledge and ideas actually become part of our skill set.

I recommend a very open and positive approach to feedback for your community. In order to reduce the anxiety often attached to feedback meetings or performance reviews, feedback needs to be a normal part of everyone's work activities. Make it clear to those in your community (and ideally in the wider organization) that seeking feedback is important and encouraged. Build a feedback culture where every person can give feedback to and receive it from any other person, regardless of where they are in the hierarchy.

An approach I personally take is to have debrief sessions after meetings or events, where everyone identifies what they felt was done well and what we as a team can improve on. We dissect parts of the conversation and reflect on the impact of certain outcomes. Doing so regularly means no one needs to be intimidated by a debrief; instead they can bring their constructive ideas.

In addition to spelling out the importance of and approach to feedback, set out some ground rules for the feedback process. For your community and within the context of the wider organization, address the following questions:

- What is a good way to ask for feedback?
- Who is the most appropriate person to seek feedback from? Is it one person, a group, the whole community?
- What should be part of a feedback conversation?
- What are some good examples of feedback, and how did it help the person receiving it to learn and improve?
- What structure should a feedback discussion have?
- What should a person avoid when giving feedback?

- Are there any formal feedback processes you want to emulate for your community?
- Can you provide any templates for specific processes?

Transparency

I am a big proponent of creating transparent systems and processes and for trusting in people's skills and expertise to get a job done rather than micromanaging them and crippling their creativity.

Creating transparency in your community brings a sense of openness. By doing so, growing the group across departments, locations, and geographies becomes much easier.

Transparency makes knowledge and information more accessible and puts responsibility and ownership on each individual to manage their work, to seek out information, and to drive their own progress. Transparency means that there is less need for management to dictate and plan every single step.

I have found that being transparent and up front about data challenges and the data strategy of your organization works particularly well with knowledge workers and especially data professionals. Why? For one, they are typically well educated and technically minded and come equipped with curiosity, investigative skills, and a desire to find answers to difficult questions. Much like journalists and researchers, data analysts and data scientists tend to do their best work when given enough freedom to explore different hypotheses and test their theories and models until they find an approach that works and that produces answers and insights. Having preconceived ideas and requests communicated in bite-sized chunks by management will not trigger particular enthusiasm from a group of intelligent, skilled people who want to extract real insights from the data.

Make it clear to the members of your community how things work, where they can find information, how they can get access to tools and systems, and who they can ask for input and help.

With transparency into these issues, preferably written down and easily accessible, people can go ahead and do their best work.

Listening

In our modern work environments in the Western world, there still is strong support for those who are most visible and who promote their ideas most loudly and enthusiastically. There also tends to be a preference for talking over listening. As analysts, data scientists, and data professionals in general, we can all gain a lot by listening more and listening better. Data do not talk back; other people do. It can be fascinating to hear their stories when we stay quiet for a little longer than we usually would and give them our full attention.

Building and fostering true listening skills takes a lot of work and is an effort every single person needs to make if they want to get better. It cannot be achieved by attending a lecture. Listening is something that needs to be practiced regularly and with intention. Listening is an important skill for fostering constructive connections in your community. It helps build long-lasting and meaningful connections between people.

I highly recommend the book *You're Not Listening* by Kate Murphy; she conveys this message much more eloquently and effectively than I ever could. Encourage those around you to read the book as well. I am confident it will result in better communication, better conversations, and a better feedback process in your community. It will help people learn to listen and will help their peers feel heard.

Through better listening and truly hearing and comprehending what others say, there are many opportunities for great ideas to come forth and make a difference for your organization, its customers, and the community it operates in.

Regular Reviews

The fourth pillar for constructive connections is to have regular reviews—reviews of processes, of projects and activities, of how people addressed an analytical challenge and tackled a problem. Similar to building transparency and establishing a feedback culture, regular reviews give you the opportunity periodically to address what is not working, to change and tweak processes, to implement new or improved steps along the way, and to hear from a diverse group of people in your community.

For our #MakeoverMonday project, we have gone through many iterations of our processes, driven by input from our community as well as our own lessons learned. I go into detail on these lessons learned in Chapter 10 and want to encourage you to consider how regular reviews can play a role in your analytics community.

- What are processes that are not working well?
- How can you address those existing issues?
- Are you aware of the issues, and, if not, who could provide information?
- At what intervals do you want to evaluate what you are doing?
- What are some quick wins you can achieve now and what are the changes that will require a more long-term solution?

Regular reviews also support your approach to creating a feedback culture because they show your willingness to change, adapt, and improve based on input from users, stakeholders, and active community members.

We have now covered the benefits of establishing and growing your analytics community. I am sure that by now you have had a few "yes, but" reactions to some of my recommendations. In Chapter 6, I focus on the risks: the things that can go wrong, that prove problematic, and throw a spanner in the works, preventing your community from being as successful as it could be.

Chapter Six

Addressing Potential Risks for Your Community

Not everyone appreciates the idea of being surrounded by people, an image that comes to mind immediately when we think of community. You might be wondering how you can ensure that the community you want to build is constructive, productive, and inclusive. And yet, whenever people work together, there is also potential for difficulties. In group settings, people can easily get distracted. There also is a risk for groupthink or, as it is more commonly described these days, for an echo chamber to form that rejects new ideas and is impacted by confirmation bias. Management and the leadership team might not buy into the idea of an analytics community and may withhold their support. And what if someone goes rogue with their own approach to the detriment of the wider community? How do you prevent and control the negative disruption and the possible destructive energy that someone can bring?

In this chapter I explore the different challenges and risks that threaten the success of your analytics communities and the potential negative impact for people. I offer suggestions for avoiding negative outcomes and for building an environment where analytics professionals can thrive, whether they flourish in a team setting or prefer to work by themselves.

Distraction

There is a genuine risk that people feel distracted from their work in a community setting that features instant communication channels, heavy reliance on social media, frequent events, and interruptions from colleagues. For truly focused work, distractions need to be minimized. How can we strike a healthy balance between fostering communities and reaping the benefits while also respecting people's need to work without distraction?

Encourage People to Share Their Preferred Working Styles

Open and transparent communication goes a long way in many situations, including when building an environment where everyone can do their best work. From my own experience, it is helpful to bring people together and openly discuss different working styles and preferences, to grow awareness and encourage others to be mindful of people's need to work without distraction.

I also recommend asking people to share the schedules they use to get work done. Some probably prefer to do a lot of focused work in the morning while others power through the afternoon. Understanding people's rhythms helps with figuring out an approach that respects the need for focused time and finding time slots during which more social activities can be scheduled.

An excellent book on the topic with several helpful recommendations for work environments is *Deep Work* by Cal Newport. I have tried many of his suggestions to see what works for me, and here are some steps I have taken to achieve a balance between deep, focused work that is essential in my day job and time for interactive, less structured engagement with the communities I am part of:

- **Scheduling time in my calendar for every task**
  In my day job, every task I am working on is scheduled in my calendar. New requests from customers, partners, or colleagues do not go on a to-do list but instead get a time slot in my calendar. To help me tackle the task immediately when the scheduled time has come, I add as many notes and ideas into the calendar event as possible, so I can dive right in.
- **Moving difficult tasks to the morning**
  I'm a morning person, so rather than avoiding a challenging task, I aim to tackle it first thing in the morning so I can stop thinking about it. Not only do I get more done this way, I also feel like I accomplished something significant before lunchtime, which boosts my mood for the entire day.

- **Removing distractions during focused time**
  When I am working on something that requires concentration and contin-ued focus, I close out my email and social communications software, set my phones to "do not disturb" and remove them from my desk. When I need to write or figure out an analytical problem, I want to get into "the zone" and truly lose myself for a few hours of deep work. I cannot accom-plish this when notifications, phone calls, and messages distract me from the task I am meant to be doing.
  This approach is something I am continuously trying to get right, because, like many people, I feel the need to always be available when at work, and the idea of ignoring all incoming communications for a few hours seems daunting. When I stick to my own rules, however, I am blown away by how much I can accomplish and how good my results are after just a few hours of dedicated focus.

- **Flexible working**
  I am a social person and I genuinely enjoy interactions with my colleagues in the office. Some of my best writing and analysis, however, happens when I am in a quiet environment, such as my home office, or a nonwork environment, like a cafe or library. Having space to think gives me better ideas and stimulates me differently. In the office, I aim to have interactions and discussions that move us forward on various topics. I coach and men-tor some of my colleagues. With others, I work on agreeing next steps for projects as well as discussing opportunities. When the time comes for me to produce strategy papers, content, proposals, and solution documents, I retreat to a space where I can reflect, pause, think, and quietly go about documenting my ideas.

I am sharing these suggestions not to have them seen as gospel but to show what works *for me* and to encourage you and your team, as well as the members of your community, to communicate openly about differ-ent approaches. Once people have a chance to share how they do their best work, setting boundaries and achieving small changes in behavior becomes a lot easier. Everyone becomes aware and can be mindful of the needs of others.

During those discussions you can also encourage people to identify the cur-rent state of distractions they are experiencing. Some of those distractions probably can be resolved, and others can be managed more effectively. There are many distractions "inflicted," on us and there are also quite a few that we introduce into our own days. Again, being aware of these distrac-tions will help people change their behaviors and will result in a less dis-tracted work environment.

If all of us can use our time at work more efficiently, we can focus on getting things done, make progress on reducing the amount of time it takes to complete tasks, and have more time available for the other things that are important to us, including family, friends, hobbies, and learning.

Groupthink/Echo Chamber

A group of like-minded people can become an echo chamber where the same opinions are multiplied and fortified, and diversity is minimized. For organizations building internal communities, it is important to address the issue of groupthink from the beginning.

This section explores different approaches for ensuring a diversity of people, skills, and opinions while also building processes, tools, and systems that foster diversity of thought, enable innovative approaches, and invite contributions from all levels.

Finding Diversity Across Your Organization

One of my mentees wanted to build her professional network and sought advice from her boss. He suggested she should talk to two people about their careers and then ask each of them to introduce her to another two people. These snowball introductions worked, and my mentee ended up speaking to dozens of people across the globe from various industries and organizations and at various stages in their career.

A similar approach can help you build a diverse analytics community in your organization. Encourage your champions to nominate two other people to include. Once they are participating, ask those two people to invite two people they know, and so on. You can do this to grow the community as a whole and when promoting your internal events, activities, and initiatives. Let your members support you and do some of the heavy lifting to grow this network.

Inviting External Input

When it comes to reducing the risk of groupthink or the formation of echo chambers, you can start small by simply bringing "outsiders"—people who currently are not part of your community—into your activities and events. Introducing business experts from different areas of your organization to the analysts and data scientists and promoting collaboration between them can lead to numerous new ideas.

Hackathons are a great way for bringing together experts from the business, the analytics department, IT, and other areas to work together on challenging questions and tasks.

Analyze Your Community

Once your community is up and running, review at regular intervals who is participating and why. Doing this will help you identify potential gaps or biases. Who is currently not represented? Are some departments missing that should be part of the initiative? Are certain people or roles overrepresented while others might miss out? Are your activities, projects, and tasks inclusive, or do they only appeal to certain people?

If, for example, most of the activities members can get involved in focus on heavily technical skills and challenges, there is less of an incentive for nontechnical people with strong business expertise to get involved. Or if gamification (which can be great fun!) is part of every single activity, people who do not want to feel pressured to compete against others, even if the competition is a friendly one, may be deterred from participating.

As you assess your community regularly, discuss your concerns with the other community leaders and champions. Seeking feedback and input from all your members via anonymous surveys can be helpful in feeling the pulse of your community and in identifying new and better ways of doing things.

Lack of Buy-in

New ideas typically are met with some resistance. In organizations, an idea like the building of an analytics community needs buy-in from management and senior leadership for long-term success. Not having management buy-in will impact effectiveness and ability to achieve meaningful outcomes. Getting approval from management and agreeing to targets and timelines for your work in building the community will help you drive successful projects and outcomes.

Data professionals usually are very passionate and enthusiastic about their work and strive to continuously improve and build their skills and knowledge. You will likely find at least a handful of people who are keen to get involved in your community and even drive and own some of the activities that help you build an environment for growth. Without the support of the leaders in your organization, however, having work seen, noticed, and recognized and achieving the true impact of data analysis across the organization likely will be a frustrating and uphill battle.

If you have not yet secured approval and support, create a clear plan to do so. (I share detailed templates for this process in Chapter 7.) Start one or two small initiatives to build momentum and achieve results that you can use to demonstrate the value your community adds to the organization.

Disruptors

People come with their knowledge, skills, and ideas. They also come with their personality, feelings, and opinions. Sometimes, unfortunately, they can disrupt a team or group through negative attitudes and/or by being dismissive, unsupportive, or downright mean and destructive. I hope that your community will be filled with people who want to contribute in the best ways and work with each other, we also have to be realistic about the potential for people to act the opposite way.

In my years of running the #MakeoverMonday project, I have enjoyed the great overall vibe of this community, with countless people participating proactively, supporting and helping each other as everyone joined the project to improve their skills in communicating effectively with data. Running #MakeoverMonday via social media also exposed the project to a number of situations that I would have rather avoided. We have had our fair share of critics, which is not a bad thing, because critiques, when done constructively, can make all of us better and have certainly pushed us to rethink processes and approaches to running the project. There have, however, been instances where discussions and debates took an unhealthy turn, which is something we always aimed to shut down as quickly and effectively as possible. In our case, our "authority" comes with the expertise we bring and the potential influence we as the leaders of the project have. The authority we have also ends right there and very much depends on the respect afforded to us by those who choose to participate. Relying on the good intentions of others makes it difficult to completely control the learning process and remove those who disrupt it.

One point people sometimes forget when they don't interact at a very personal level is that behind every question, every draft report, or first version of a dashboard is an analyst, data scientist, or subject matter expert who is also a person with feelings. The importance of being respectful with one another, to follow rules and guidelines, and to bring understanding and empathy to the communities we are part of cannot be underestimated.

Be ready with a plan for how to deal with people who disrupt your community in negative ways. You cannot foresee every possible outcome, but having rules of engagement that people must follow to participate gives you a framework for assessing people's behavior. Within your organization, you can engage with the human resources department to discuss potential conflict situations and how to handle them before they arise.

Whether the attacks come online or in person, few if any of us enjoy having to defend ourselves or having to break up a fight between others. Setting clear ground rules can help but will not guarantee that those situations will not arise.

Now that we have discussed the benefits of building an internal analytics community, why they are important and helpful for people to do their best work, and what some of the risks are that you want to be prepared for and able to avoid, it is time to look at the how. Next I share my recommendations, tips, templates, and guidelines for starting and building your community.

Chapter Seven

Practical Guides
for Getting Started

By now you are probably keen to get started, take some actions, and see a few quick results in your organization. In the following pages I give you several suggestions of what to do *right now* if you want to make a start or kick off the next phase for your analytics community. I also pose a number of questions, because every community is at a different point of maturity, so there is no one-size-fits-all solution. At the end of the chapter, following the description of different activities, are a number of templates you can use, take as guidance, and adjust to run events and plan your next steps.

Purpose and Mission

Without wanting to curb your enthusiasm to roll up your sleeves and get started, I want to begin by addressing the question of purpose and mission, because this will guide what you do next.

What is the purpose of the community you are building? Perhaps it fits one of the following descriptions:

- Our community is intended to enable knowledge sharing between and upskilling of our employees.
- Our community's purpose is to break down silos and enable better collaboration.
- Our community will help us showcase our expertise to the wider industry.
- Our community will spread the adoption of data-driven decision making across the business.

Maybe your community ticks a few or all of these boxes. Or you have a different purpose altogether. It is important to be clear on that purpose and to communicate it to community members and your leadership.

Make sure you know what you want to achieve for the organization as a whole. Along with focusing on the community itself, focus on the impact the community will have on the business and the bottom line: How will it benefit your customers, partners, suppliers, and others? What is your mission?

What about the people in your community? What is the benefit for them to be a part of the community? I shared my thoughts on how communities benefit their members in Chapter 4. Maybe you have additional ideas on how you want your colleagues and fellow data professionals to benefit from their involvement in the analytics community you are building.

Finally, when considering your purpose and goals, think about how you will measure success. When looking back at your efforts and those of the people working with you, in a few months, one year from now or further in the future, how will you know that you have achieved your goals and your mission? What are some tangible metrics you can use to track your progress along the way? What can be measured easily? What is less concrete and may need to be observed and qualified in different ways?

Once you have gone through the exercise of tackling these questions, it is time to consider the structure of your community.

Structure

Building a community from scratch is an exciting endeavor, and having a blank canvas gives you plenty of opportunity to lay the right foundations.

If you already have things in place, you probably also have lessons learned, and the next suggestions can give you some ideas for what you can add, change, or improve.

Looking at the structure of your community, first evaluate what you already have.

- What are the systems you currently work with?
- What tools are in place?
- What are the organizational and departmental structures you are working with?
- Where are the people located who should be part of your community? Are there geographical challenges to overcome?

The structure you establish should serve the community **right now** while also accommodating future growth, with more people and teams becoming part of it, across locations and languages.

Considering what your community should look like in three months, nine months, or even two years from today will help you plan ahead.

- How many people are (going to be) part of your community right now?
- How quickly do you want to grow? Is there a roll-out plan for analytics tools that accompanies the growth, or is the plan more focused on tasks and people?
- Is the community open to members from all parts of the business from the beginning, or will you invite people department by department?
- Do you want your community to go further than training and development and become a differentiator for your organization when it comes to hiring people, gaining a competitive advantage, and making an impact on the market?

There are many more questions you can consider, and revisiting them regularly will help you assess whether you are on track to achieve your goals. Some answers might be dictated by management. It is important to have leadership buy-in and support to establish communities that are sustainable in the long term, are successful, and make a difference to the participants as well as the wider organization.

In terms of practical and task-driven aspects, it is helpful to work through the list of immediate and longer-term targets for the specific tasks and outputs you want to drive through the community. Having a tangible list of goals for your analysts, data scientists, and business experts to work on collaboratively and with the help of the community structures ensures that aside from training, development, and networking, there is also a focus on producing specific outputs that are needed right now.

Processes

The people you bring together will need to establish new processes over time, driven by tasks, requirements, tools, and the needs of the community members. There are likely to be several existing processes currently used for data analysis, reporting, and visualization that can be improved. These range from requirements gathering, to data load and preparation, to analytical frameworks and approaches as well as visual analysis and reporting.

How people go about their analysis, the challenges they face and hurdles they need to overcome when working with data are not trivial. A common problem is gaining access to data that is critical for analysis. Analysts might also struggle to get licenses for the right tools to do their work, or certain review processes may be cumbersome and lengthy. Once you bring people together through your community, there is a great opportunity to have them address these issues and propose solutions. They have probably thought about different approaches many times, at least whenever they faced a specific challenge.

I want to urge you to make it possible for your community members to highlight the processes that need improvement so data professionals and subject matter experts can do their work more effectively. Even if you cannot address every issue right now, it is important to have these conversations, achieve some quick wins, and then ensure the more challenging problems are solved step-by-step over time. Doing so can help you alleviate process issues that hinder progress, delay timelines, frustrate people, and lead to tension between teams and departments. Identifying, documenting, and finding solutions that address bottlenecks in current processes and highlight dependencies between processes, individual people, and teams is an excellent way to drive positive outcomes through your community.

When people are able to collaborate and communicate in new and improved ways, they find many solutions to existing problems.

People

Depending on the size of your organization, you probably know some, if not all of the people who should be involved in building, growing, and developing your internal analytics community. If you are building the community in a grassroots effort, who would you like to have as part of the first phase? Who are some of the champions in your organization who are interested and engaged already around data and analytics? Are they data experts already, or does your selection also include subject matter experts whom you want to involve more in data analysis, visualization, and reporting? And if you have an existing community that you want to grow, shape, and further develop, what gaps are there? Who is currently not included and how can you address this?

Your people are the backbone and core of your community. They are what makes it actually a community. The rest is just infrastructure, systems, and processes that enable them. Having champions in your community who will drive activities, projects, and initiatives is important so others can group around them, contribute, and also become champions in their own right. It is likely that *you* are one of those champions, but perhaps due to your current role and the commitments it comes with, you cannot drive as much activity as others.

Being the enabler behind the scenes, bringing ideas, providing support, and being a spokesperson among senior leadership are essential roles and make you a key part of the community.

Activities

Once you have selected some people for your community and others join them and you have your existing systems and processes, what do you actually want them to focus on? Do you want your community primarily to drive training and development activities to support members in building their skills? Or is there a large departmental or even organization-wide analytics project to deliver?

An important consideration here is how data literate the people in your organization already are. Is there a baseline of knowledge, which means everyone can get started working on specific tasks and outcomes? Or do you need to create this baseline through training first?

Understanding, listing, and reviewing the priorities for this community can help you identify how to proceed. If your organization already has an established community that you want to grow further, this is an opportunity to review how people currently work together, how activities are prioritized, and how tasks are distributed. If most of this happens in an ad hoc fashion, there is room to introduce some structure that utilizes existing dynamics and people's momentum and aligns it to the organization's goals and needs.

Here are some examples of activities that you might already be running or could be doing in the future. This list is supported by templates for selected activities at the end of the chapter.

Training and Development

When it comes to training, these activities can help build technical, analytical, and communication skills in your people:

- **Introduction to statistics:** Teach people the fundamental principles of statistics.
- **Tool-specific training:** Teach people how to work with analytics software, data visualization software, and statistical packages.
- **Analytical framework:** Give people an approach for analysis they can apply to any analytical challenge and that allows them to progress in a structured way through their analysis.
- **Best practices:** Share best practices on topics ranging from technical, to visualization and communication approaches as well as business expertise, in structured and focused sessions.
- **Communicating with data:** Give people the methodologies and tools for effectively visualizing and reporting their findings.

Collaborative Challenges

Most people I have met in the analytics industry enjoy being given a challenge. These can range from data visualization challenges, such as #MakeoverMonday, to hackathons where the most insightful outcome wins. And their participation is not just about competing and winning but rather giving individuals or teams a question for which they need to find an answer.

Humans love riddles and puzzles and having to figure out solutions. Using challenges to motivate your people can be an effective approach for tackling specific problems or questions in short bursts of activity while also creating a stimulating environment for participants.

- **Data visualization challenges** encourage people to review existing reports and visualizations and make them more effective and user-friendly through changes to formatting, layout, and messaging.
- **Hackathons** bring together people internally (and potentially include external experts) to solve a specific problem or find answers to a specific question.
- **Regular highlights** reward people's contributions that are exceptional and set a high standard for everyone to aspire to.

Meetups

Meetups are an excellent way to connect individual members in your community and can facilitate problem-solving sessions, technical support, and mentoring. You can establish both in-person meetups as well as virtual sessions and include a structured agenda or run them more like open-door office hours.

With both options, I recommend having regular times that people can put in their calendar. In my experience, this consistency and reliability is a key factor in growing a community, because it allows people to come together regularly while also enabling new members to join easily. They can simply attend one of these recurring meetups and become part of the group.

To make your meetup most valuable for participants, try any of these suggestions:

- **Office hours:** People can drop in during a set 60- or 90-minute time slot to meet with and get help from experts (e.g., to work on an analytical question, a technical problem, or to get feedback on their work).
- **Lunch & learn sessions:** Schedule regular, say every two week, sessions over lunch where people can present the topics they are working on, the solutions they have developed, or share ideas from external events, conferences, and training.
- **Formal knowledge sharing:** Select a specific topic or tool that brings like-minded people together for learning. This could be a quarterly meetup where internal and external experts share their knowledge relating to the analytics software and tools used internally, best practices, and analytical approaches.

Internal Conferences

If you are beginning to establish your community, a full conference might seem impossible to achieve. Internal conferences are not, however, so far-fetched, and they are opportunities to bring people together, facilitate training, and share with the wider organization how data and analytics support decision-making processes.

For those who are ready to set up an internal conference for their community and their organization, here are some ideas of what to include. The templates section at the end of this chapter features a sample schedule for a one-day conference.

Planning your conference:

- **Keynotes:** Include one or two keynote sessions that inspire your community, highlight the importance of data and analytics, and inject fresh ideas for how to approach work. These can be given by senior management or an executive, and I suggest considering an external speaker.
- **Best practices:** Have a session on the agenda that highlights best practices for analytics. It can include analysis and analytical methods, data visualization, and different approaches for communicating with data based on your business, or very specific topics, such as predictive modeling approaches, color choices, and corporate design guidelines.
- **Technical deep-dives:** Bring people together around their areas of expertise. You might want to include sessions that address specific statistical packages, analytical techniques, or dashboard design, for example. These sessions give people a chance to build their skills, learn something new, and take fresh ideas with them into their day job.
- **Workshops:** Include one or two hands-on sessions if possible. Again, people can learn something or experiment with a new software. You can also use this time to bring together businesspeople, analysts, and data engineers to tackle a specific challenge or business requirement within a set time frame.
- **Showcases and demo stations:** Depending on your venue, you might have space for showcase stations. Having the people who work with data every day present interactive demos can be a way to bring a deeper understanding of the value of data analysis to business departments.

Online Portal

Your community will create many outputs and deliverables over time. They will also develop content, examples, templates, guides, and manuals. All of these items are invaluable for the ongoing growth of your community as well as for use by the wider business. How do you capture all of this information? Many organizations have content in several places, with different levels of access, meaning that people may or may not get to see the content they are looking for.

One way to address this issue is to host all content being created on a portal that everyone can access. I do not mean clunky shared drives where people upload files that no one ever uses because no one knows what they contain. Instead, portals based on user-friendly, customizable collaboration platforms should be dynamic and create an inviting environment where people *want* to participate.

Some considerations for an online portal include these:

- What kind of content do your community members create and share?
  - **Blogs and how-to-guides** can be embedded in a browser-based content management tool or internal blog interface.
  - **Interactive visualizations and dashboards** will require some connection to the sharing platform where they are hosted and can be embedded through iframes, making them part of a page and more accessible to a wider audience.
  - **Templates, manuals, and scripts** should be available to a broad user base to help people work more effectively and efficiently and to ensure governance approaches are followed.
- How do you want people to interact?
  - **Instant messaging tools** let people contact others when they have questions, need help, or want feedback. These tools, however, can also be distracting and a source of regular interruptions, so implementing and using them will require guidelines and governance. In my experience, they are far more efficient than email and drive communication between colleagues who are geographically dispersed and located across different time zones.
  - **Online forums** are an excellent format for people to ask and answer questions and attach examples, screen shots, and solutions while also being searchable platforms where content is kept within the context

of these Q&A-style discussions. Depending on your organization's size, adding an internal forum platform may not be feasible, but it could be a solution in the future. For larger organizations, this internal platform can indeed be an extremely valuable tool for sharing ideas and knowledge and addressing many questions that might otherwise require a support service and more time-consuming processes.

- Is your online portal also your publishing platform for content?
  - ◆ Will end users **access reports, dashboards, and analyses** through this portal? Bringing all content into one place can help with establishing data analysis as a core process for every function of the business. It also means that the user interface will need to cater to different user personas with their unique needs for information, support, and news.
  - ◆ Do you have a way to structure the portal so that **content is categorized** neatly? Making the portal structure intuitive and easily visible reduces barriers to entry and can drive higher engagement across the organization. If you want them to really use information, it is important to make accessing and finding information as easy as possible.
  - ◆ Does your current or planned portal solution have **good search functionality**? Many users are accustomed to using search rather than navigating around to find their answers. Having good search functionality that returns the most relevant results is important as the amount of content on your portal grows and develops.

Diego Parker

Diego found a job working as an analytics consultant. During his application process he received a lot of help via online forums. He wanted to give back and help others in the same way he had been supported. Diego tirelessly answered questions on Tableau's community forums, ranking in the top 70 forum participants globally.

Diego says he learned a lot by answering questions, having to make sure that his explanations and examples are easy for people to understand and apply. He also learned about different use cases, how people utilize data and analytics in different industries and at different organizations. He gained the highest level of certification for Tableau Desktop mainly through his consistent engagement on the forums.

Source: Diego Parker

Evaluating a portal solution requires a comprehensive process to take into account your organization's unique requirements. The listed considerations are intended to guide you on some user needs when it comes to analytics content, sharing, and collaboration that will also support your internal community.

Online forums offer great benefits for those consuming the content, but they also benefit the people who make the effort to answer questions, as we can see from the example of Diego Parker.

Templates

This section contains several specific how-to guides, templates, and practical recommendations you can immediately put into action. My intention with this book is not just to inspire people to create, build, and grow communities at some point but to do something **right now**, no matter how mature data and analytics are in your organization.

Small Events and Short Activities (< 3 hours)

First up are small events and activities that require less than 3 hours of time commitment from participants. You can likely organize these quickly and with a minimal budget as you can utilize existing facilities, systems, and tools.

#MakeoverMonday Live Session

Over the past several years I have witnessed time and time again how useful an exercise it is to take existing dashboards and reports and give them a makeover. The focus is not on changing everything but rather on making what is there more user-friendly, easier to understand, and more engaging and ensuring the key messages, insights, and findings are communicated clearly.

Essentially, the makeover involves an improvement of the visuals, with typical changes including simplification (e.g., colors, shapes, icons, etc.), formatting, rewording, layout improvements, and the use of more appropriate charts.

In #MakeoverMonday live sessions, people come together to work on a specific dashboard or visualization and do so either individually, in pairs, or as teams. The exercise is time-bound to ensure people focus on truly quick wins and do not overengineer and overcomplicate their work. It is very helpful to have participants present their work at the end of the session to share the different approaches and results with the entire group.

Here is how you can run a #MakeoverMonday live session.

What You Will Need

- If you want people to create the makeovers during this session, you will need a room large enough for everyone to work comfortably on their computers at tables. I recommend this hands-on approach because it allows for taking action immediately and is more effective than writing a list of changes and asking one person to make them later.

- Wi-Fi, power outlets, a large screen for people to present to, perhaps snacks and beverages (these are always well received by participants).

- A dashboard or visualization that needs improvements. I recommend sticking to a single makeover rather than attempting to work on multiple dashboards in a short amount of time. It is more effective to work collectively on a single item than to try to cover many different ones without achieving the desired results. The original dashboard might come from your team, but if it is owned by another part of the business, ensure to get their buy-in into the entire process, so that any changes you work on and propose will actually get implemented.

- About 2 hours of everyone's time.

Recommended Session Structure

- Personal introductions (10 minutes). Depending on whether people know each other yet, start with brief introductions, so everyone knows everyone else.

- Topic and session objective introduction
  - What does the dashboard look like?
  - What is it about?
  - Is there a data dictionary in case people are not familiar with the underlying data and terminology?
  - State the purpose of the session: What do you want to achieve?
  - State the time limit.

- Hands-on makeover (60–90 minutes)
  - Get people to work individually, in pairs, or in groups, putting people together who typically don't work together to encourage fresh ideas and to help them form new connections inside the organization.
  - Set a timer for 60 to 90 minutes, depending on how much time you want to allocate for the session.
  - Point out who the subject matter experts are in case people have questions.

- Set expectations around what people should do (e.g., should they save/publish their finished work somewhere on an internal portal? Or is there a submission process whereby outputs are collected?).

- Presentations (20 minutes)
  - Ask as many people as time permits to share their results with the group.
  - Discuss as a group and invite people to ask questions of the presenter and provide constructive feedback.
  - Note: This is not the time when people should list the various reasons why a certain approach will not work. The session is intended to be for practicing effective ways to communicate data and information. After 60 to 90 minutes, a dashboard will likely not be perfect yet. You will, however, see several different approaches to improving it, and they can be effective starting points for making various changes.

- Next steps
  - What will happen with the outputs people created? Ensure you have some clear next steps for what will happen with their contributions.
  - Ensure the owners of the original dashboard or visualization can now implement the recommended changes to improve their work. It is important to provide the results to the business unit or team that has ownership of the original.
  - Arrange another makeover session. Ask people about what they learned in the session. Run these kinds of meetings regularly to improve existing dashboards and visualizations one week at a time. Doing so also helps to communicate and teach best practices to a larger group of people over time, so that you will see an improvement in the quality of visualizations across the business.

Alternatives

- If you are unable to use an existing dashboard or visualization from the business, consider joining the public #MakeoverMonday project (MakeoverMonday.co.uk) and run these in-person sessions using one of our data sets.

- The data we use is all publicly available. Using the in-person session to discuss limitations of the existing visualization while also identifying what works well, before creating makeovers, is a great way to improve people's critical analysis and feedback skills while giving them a chance to regularly hone their technical and communication skills.

Internal User Group

Whether people are experts for a specific subject or are brought together based on using a certain tool or software, user groups can build connections between people who have something in common. People who make it to an expert level typically are passionate about what they do, about their knowledge and the detailed technical and intellectual intricacies of solving problems as part of their job. They tend to enjoy exchanging their ideas with like-minded people, and some of them are ready to present their findings and knowledge to a wider audience.

Setting up an internal user group—for example, for all data scientists, based on the topics of analysis using R and Python—makes use of people's willingness to give, combined with their interest and expertise in the given topic. It is also a way to introduce new employees, community members, or team members to others or to a new software or to help them learn about a topic.

Internal user groups, much like public user groups, should follow a consistent approach, so that people find it easier and less daunting to make their participation a habit. What could an internal user group look like for your organization? Here is a sample agenda for a user group focused on data analysis and visualization. Feel free to amend and adapt it to your needs.

What You Will Need

- A venue big enough to accommodate everyone.
- A large screen or projector for presentations as well as a microphone and lectern, connector cables, and adapters.
- Theater-style seating, a big round table, or any other room setup depending on your audience size and the presentations and activities you would like to include.
- Snacks and beverages, depending on the time of day and the duration of your user group. Providing some food and drinks always seems to help people to relax and get comfortable while listening to other people's presentations.

Recommended Session Structure

- Introductions
  - Welcome people to the user group.
  - Set expectations and run through housekeeping details and timing.
  - Introduce speakers.

- Presentations/Talks
  - Keep these to a maximum of 30 minutes per speaker.
  - A good approach is to have a variety of topics, including a business-focused presentation, a technical presentation, and a hands-on session. Doing this ensures that people grow their business knowledge, their technical understanding of specific concepts or technologies, and have the opportunity to apply what they have learned about in a hands-on session to increase their technical skills.
  - Other styles of presentations can include panel discussions with Q&A, group discussions and exercises, and keynotes that introduce external speakers to inspire your audience.
  - As a suggestion for external speakers, why not invite a customer, vendor, or supplier to present to your community?
  - Include short breaks either between each talk (5 minutes) or a slightly longer break (15 minutes) before the hands-on session.
- Next steps
  - Include a call to action. I always recommend this step so people walk out of the meeting with practical recommendations and the ability to turn their new knowledge into applicable skills.
  - Share how people can connect with speakers and where they can find additional resources.
  - Announce the next user group, so people have plenty of notice and can add it to their calendars before their schedules fill with other commitments.
  - Invite others to speak next time.

Alternatives

If an in-person user group is not feasible because people are too geographically dispersed or cannot all meet in the same place at the given time, consider hosting a virtual user group.

- A virtual user group will require a different setup, ensuring very high audio and video quality for video conferencing as well as having every participant able to use the required software to join.
- To ensure maximum reach and participation, remember time zone differences.
- Speakers need to adjust their talks to ensure slides are effective in their balance of content and visuals and communicate ideas clearly. This applies to virtual as well as in-person events.

- Setting some ground rules during the virtual user group (e.g., Q&A at the end of each talk, all participants must be muted during a talk, etc.) is important for it to run smoothly.
- Having a place where resources are shared after the session will help drive participants to the necessary content.

Weekly Office Hours

Providing your colleagues and your internal community with set weekly office hours can be a helpful way to start one-on-one training and to have a way to address questions and solve problems quickly. This does not mean *you* have to be the person fielding all the requests. It could be done by an individual or by a group of people, and even those people can change every week.

Weekly office hours can relate to general inquiries and to specific software questions or analytical challenges. Bringing experts and experienced data professionals together and making their expertise accessible to the wider audience in a structured and time-bound format ensures people can get the help they want, and those providing the help are not inundated with constant requests and can focus their time on these weekly sessions.

What You Will Need

- A small room, ideally the same room each week, with desks, Wi-Fi access and chairs, so people can sit down while talking through their questions.
- Any number of people with expertise and experience on the topics that are likely to come up, such as data preparation and access, how to use specific tools or software, statistical analysis, how to present and communicate findings most effectively, building dashboards, and the like.
- A communication channel through which you can announce office hours, location, list the people available during the session and potentially also collect questions ahead of time.

Recommended Session Structure

- Allow for 60 to 90 minutes, if people can make that much time available. It is good to strike a balance between having enough time to address people's questions and also not placing too high a demand on the time of experts. (Sixty minutes per week is likely to be much more effective than 90 minutes twice a month.)
- Get people to drop by at any point during the allocated time. If there is a wait, encourage them to chat with others who are waiting; they might be able to resolve their problem with their peers.

- Arrange for follow-up actions.
  - What are the next steps in case the issue is not resolved?
  - If the issue was resolved, request that the person who brought the issue forward writes up the problem statement and the solution and shares it internally. Chances are others are having the same or similar questions. By producing these solutions and sharing them internally—for example, in a forum or messaging platform—the entire community can access the information and learn (and also thank those giving up their time each week to help).

Alternatives

- If an in-person weekly session is not yet feasible for your organization or is impractical due to people's availability and location, try a virtual session for which people submit their questions ahead of time. During the webinar, one or multiple experts address the questions. You can record the webinar and share the content after each session.
- Depending on your current setup, you might also have access to external experts to facilitate these weekly or biweekly office hours. Bring in people from the industry and experienced data analysis professionals to help with some of the topics. You can also seek the support of vendors of analytics software to address technical questions related to the tools you use.

Internal Conference

A number of organizations that have established data analytics communities run internal conferences for their analysts and data professionals. Making these conferences effective is easier with established processes, tools, a group of people to draw on, and several topics that can be used for presentations and discussion rounds. This does not mean that a smaller organization cannot or should not aim to run an internal conference. The format of a conference, whether it is a half-day or full-day event, may lend itself more to a larger community, however.

Conferences can be set up as an extension of a user group, adding external speakers, additional sessions, and a keynote, as well as break times for networking and meals. An internal conference can drive people's engagement and motivation, trigger new connections and collaborations, and help people see their role in the overall organization and its data-driven strategy. It can further signal the importance of analytics to the wider organization as well as the external market.

What You Will Need

- A venue big enough to accommodate all your attendees for the sessions throughout the day. Consider whether everyone will present in the same room. Having everyone in the same venue will make logistics easier and may also require some compromises on room size, depending on what you can access.

- A schedule with sessions to fill out the day, as well as the necessary speakers to run each session.

- Catering for breakfast and lunch as well as refreshments throughout the day.

- A list of everyone you want to invite and a channel to promote the event from about six weeks prior to the conference (or longer if people are required to travel to attend).

- Audio and video equipment, including various adapters for people's laptops.

- Streaming/broadcasting capabilities if employees have the option to attend virtually from other locations.

- A timetable for planning, with deadlines for submissions, agenda, registrations, and the like.

Recommended Structure for the Day

- I recommend starting between 9:30 and 10:00 AM, to allow people to arrive, get settled, and handle any urgent calls before the conference kicks off. If your organization or your office has a schedule that differs from the typical 9 to 5 time frame, adjust your start times accordingly.

- To set the scene, have a keynote of no more than 30 minutes to help people get in the right headspace for the upcoming sessions. This keynote can be done by an internal speaker (e.g., someone from the executive team) or an external speaker (ideally someone who is a known entity in the industry). The keynote sets the tone for the day, so be deliberate in choosing the right person, someone who will energize people, motivate them, and make them feel excited about the day ahead and the role they play in its success.

- Following the keynote, you have room for two sessions before the lunch break. Giving people a 5-minute break between these two sessions can help them focus throughout the morning.

  - A mix of technical, analytical, and business topics is a good way to address a broad audience.

  - Encourage your speakers to introduce several examples that make each topic tangible and memorable.

- ◆ Showing new insights and findings from their analysis can also be a good way for speakers to drive discussions.

- Break for lunch around 12:30 PM. An hour lunch break might seem like a long time, but the break gives attendees a chance to network, eat, discuss the previous talks, and get some fresh air before the afternoon sessions.

- For the afternoon, I recommend adding a hands-on session where people can learn and be actively engaged. This will help to get over the postlunch fatigue and break things up a little from the more lecture-style approach of the morning.

- Why not finish the day with a panel discussion? Adding a session at the end of the day that drives discussions, challenges people a little, and encourages them to engage will leave them with many ideas to take away. Depending on the size of your audience, it can be useful to include attendees in the discussion through questions, live polling, or a short quiz.

- A nice way to finish the day is to provide another networking opportunity. Note that this should be optional so as to not encroach on people's personal lives too much. Finishing the sessions around 4:30 PM gives everyone an opportunity to spend a bit of time at the end of the afternoon to discuss the day, their impressions and ideas, and to outline the actions they may take from what they learned.

Overall, there is plenty of flexibility in how to design an internal conference around data and analytics. Your audience size, the type of people who will attend, and their needs and those of the organization will largely determine what content you should focus on. Experimenting and learning from other events, such as internal user groups and weekly office hours, will inform your plans for a full-day event and will let you test out how different topics are received.

Alternatives

- Running a full-day virtual conference may not be the easiest thing to do, but it is certainly possible and something to consider if it makes it easier for you and your analytics community to get an event off the ground and assemble speakers and attendees.

  One example of a full-day virtual conference organized by a community that spans four different locations/time zones each year is the Tableau Fringe Festival (TFF). It was started by Emily Kund to provide a platform for speakers from the Tableau community who did not have the opportunity to speak at the annual Tableau Conference. TFF is an independently organized event that focuses on bringing together a diverse range of speakers with interesting topics and high-quality content.

Sessions are between 20 and 45 minutes in duration and cover technical topics, professional development, brand building, community projects, and best practices. The agenda is packed from morning to evening, facilitated by volunteers in each of the four locations: Asia Pacific, Europe/ Middle East/Africa, Latin America, and North America. Anyone is able to submit a speaker application, presenting a topic related to Tableau, and sessions are recorded and made available after the event.

The benefit of a virtual, free event is that participants can attend the sessions they are interested in from the comfort of their desk or their home, without the need to travel or free up an entire day, while also receiving high-quality content live streamed to them.

You can find out more at thefringefestival.rocks.

Hackathons

Hackathons as a way of getting more value out of existing data are becoming increasingly popular with organizations. Hackathons are events where people from different areas of expertise come together to solve challenges around data, software, coding, analysis, or statistical modeling. A hackathon might have a clear objective communicated through specific questions, or it can allow participants and teams to choose their own adventure.

For data analysis hackathons, both approaches have their benefits. Focusing participants on a specific set of questions may result in clear answers and next steps. This might come at the expense of additional insights, though, which are more likely to happen when people have the flexibility to explore and follow their intuition. Giving people such flexibility and asking them to come up with insights without clear direction can be challenging, but it's also a blank slate for people to tackle the data without any preconceived ideas.

Hackathons at the German Football Association

For Pascal Bauer, data scientist for the German national soccer team, the availability of data is making unstoppable technological progress in almost all domains. The German National Team has a lot of data, ranging from tracking players' pathway on the field and their performance in training to a digital reproduction of every professional football match at a centimeter-level of detail (1 cm = 0.4 in).

Benefiting from the affordability of computing power and the development of machine learning models by a whole research sector for the past

70 years, Pascal sees a huge potential for soccer. Other industries as well as other sports, such as baseball and basketball, have proven that the integration of data-driven decision making within organizations is useful. At least for the last two years the tracking technologies in soccer have been accurate enough to do tactical match analysis based on the data, opening up a whole new research area: applied data science for tactical match analysis in professional football.

In 2020, the German National Team and Under-20 National Team qualified for top international competitions (UEFA EURO 2020, the 2020 Summer Olympics in Tokyo, U-20 Women's World Cup, which have all been postponed to 2021 due to COVID-19) that require frequent play with matches usually played twice a week. Similarly, as a result of its success in the German Bundesliga, Eintracht Frankfurt, a top-tier German soccer club, qualified for the Europa League the last two seasons. For example, in 2019, Eintracht faced 56 international opponents and played more official matches than any other team in Europe other than Liverpool Football Club with 58.

This frequency of play creates several recurring challenges for match analysis staff because every opponent must be analyzed in detail within a very short amount of time. While the application of data science has supported many domains in other industries by automating recurring processes, the same potential has yet to be exploited in professional football, even when data are available. There are two problems: Match analysts do not have the skill set to handle the 10 million data points per match, and qualified data scientists who do have the required technical skills often do not have access to the data and/or do not know how to ask the right questions.

Pascal and his team have launched a series of hackathons to address and solve the most prevalent challenges in soccer. Over the course of three months, teams of two—one data scientist and one match analyst—combine their respective expertise to find the best solution to soccer's data-related problems. To create the best environment for success, each team is assigned a pair of mentors with professional experience in machine learning and soccer, respectively.

The idea for the hackathon developed over time to close the gap between soccer expertise and data expertise. Pascal and his team recognized this gap, which was further supported by benchmarks that showed that other leagues and national soccer clubs were far more advanced with the integration of data-driven approaches into their organizations than German Bundesliga clubs. Since decision makers in Bundesliga clubs usually do not have a STEM background, it can be difficult to create the necessary awareness for this new area and to persuade them to hire data scientists into their coaching teams. The data science community, in contrast, is very open-minded and often willing to apply their competencies to new and exciting data sets and topics.

Pascal and his colleagues wanted to help provide the necessary connections to Bundesliga clubs and enable them to get a better idea of what they could use data for. Facilitating a common understanding between the sports experts and the data experts is not without challenges.

In Pascal's experience, the biggest challenge is to actually "speak the same language." The biggest lesson learned from their first hackathon was that participants certainly do not have the same perspective on a question or challenge. For a successful data science application in professional soccer, you need a data-literate practitioner (e.g., coach, match analyst, etc.) and a data scientist with a basic understanding of the sport. Having both is very rare, so Pascal and his team tried putting people together in a room and letting them work on a challenge. With people excited and motivated to participate, they started understanding each other and actually produced interesting and insightful results.

The community that Pascal and his team have nurtured over the course of three years is diverse and has brought new people into the domain of sports analytics while broadening the horizon for coaching staff in regard to data. Although most of the information and data for professional soccer stays within a small subset of people, there are nevertheless many opportunities to communicate the topics of analytics and data to people.

Germany has had a significant need for data science education for the past years. The German Football Association has become involved, for example, through university classes, where they explain the basic concepts of machine learning to students based on soccer-specific use cases and examples. Whether students love soccer or not, having such a familiar topic to work with can be an exciting way to learn mathematical concepts.

What is next for Pascal, his team, and their hackathon initiatives? The hackathon is currently provided as a service to German Bundesliga clubs. The team wants to engage with the public too. In the medium to long term, the goal is to come up with a curriculum for data scientists in soccer and for data-literate match analysts. Pascal and his team are working closely together with several universities to integrate data science basics into sport science degrees and to provide data and use cases for data science courses.

Source: Pascal Bauer

If you want to run a hackathon internally or externally, I suggest having a few questions for participants to explore so that they have some direction. Then give them the additional flexibility to go down any unexplored paths they might discover during their analyses. Hackathons need a considerable amount of planning and preparation but are also fun and engaging events that help solve problems and establish new connections between colleagues and potentially external experts.

What You Will Need

- It is important to be clear on the objective of the hackathon. What do you want to achieve? What questions are you seeking answers for?

- People typically work in pairs or teams to ensure diversity of skill sets and business knowledge. I recommend bringing together those with data expertise (preparation, transformation, etc.), those with business knowledge (subject matter experts), and those with data visualization and communication skills. Each team needs to have the skills to cover the various processes and steps that lead to the desired outcomes.

- The venue could be a single large room with group tables that are positioned separately from one another or a collaborative space where teams can find quiet areas for working and discussing.

- Establish an agenda as well as a clear communication plan ahead of time, including invitations to participants and ongoing communication in the lead-up to the hackathon and after the event.

- There are a few more things to consider ahead of time:

  - What data will people work with? Making the data available ahead of time helps participants familiarize themselves with the data so they can use their time at the event more effectively.

- Will the data be prepared for participants? I highly recommend you provide them with as clean and complete a data set as possible, so the experts who spend their day at the hackathon to tackle questions can focus on doing that rather than on data preparation.
- If external people are participating, you will need a process for them to sign nondisclosure agreements before the event if they work with confidential data.
- What is the technical setup for the hackathon? Will everyone bring their own laptop to work or are you providing laptops? Are there enough power outlets, a stable Wi-Fi connection, as well as screens for presentations available?
- What is the reward for participating? A small but meaningful prize goes a long way in motivating people. After all, these are competitive people.
- What will happen after the event? People typically want to know whether their contributions made a difference. Give them an idea of the next steps and the results farther down the track, if possible.
- Food and beverages for participants throughout the day.

Recommended Structure for the Day

- Opening remarks
  - Tell people why their expertise is required to solve the challenges.
- Introduction to the challenge and questions
  - What questions do you want participants to tackle?
  - Are there any particular things they should know about the data?
  - Who is their target audience for the results?
- Time for teams to work
  - Allow for several hours so people can get their work done and find new insights and solutions.
  - Ensure people have places to sit or stand and collaborate throughout the day.
- Presentations
  - Each team will present and explain their results. Depending on the number of teams, these presentations typically range from 5 to 10 minutes for each team plus time for Q&A by the stakeholders or judging panel.
- Closing remarks, awards, and prizes
  - What happens next? How will people's work help the organization?
  - Award prizes for participation and of course a special prize to the winning team.

Alternatives

Running a full-day hackathon for several, if not dozens of, participants is a great challenge and typically a lot of fun for participants. It also requires a fair bit of work and may not be feasible for your organization at this point. Perhaps you could consider a small hackathon-style session?

- You can run "mini hacks" like the #MakeoverMonday live session discussed earlier. The focus is on the specific questions you have around data and analysis rather than the aesthetics of dashboards.
- Allow around 2 to 2.5 hours for a mini hack. Set out the expectations and some guidelines ahead of time around how the session will run and get a handful of people in the room.
- Working with a sprint-style approach on a particular business question or problem can give you quick results that can be refined afterward and also allow you to fail fast, discovering the ways something does not work, which in turn helps you to figure out better approaches.

Training Sessions

Training sessions are valuable activities that can be done regularly and can be open to a variety of community members. Providing and organizing internal training for people in your organization provides benefits beyond building skills and knowledge. It also gives participants an opportunity to recognize each other's talents, support one another, and mentor others. In addition, regular training means there are frequent activities for people to get involved in and new employees can more easily find their way around.

The content of the training you offer depends on the needs of your organization as well as the people available to teach. Over time you will evolve the curriculum and include more and more topics. To get started, I suggest gathering a list of potential topics and the names of people who could teach. Topics will likely focus on specific technical themes, such as the use of particular analytical software, dashboard design best practices, communicating with data, and analytical methods and frameworks. Consider also including training for soft skills, such as stakeholder management, presentation and demonstration skills, and requirements gathering.

The training sessions can, of course, also be facilitated by an external trainer. Depending on your audience size and budget, adding external experts as teachers and trainers will be a great way to introduce new and other ideas to your community as well as offering specialist courses to your colleagues.

What You Will Need

- A suitable location, such as a training room in-house, a conference room, or an offsite venue where you can host the training.
- A list of topics and trainers to facilitate each session.
- Participants: You may want to offer sessions selectively or make them open for everyone to sign up on a first-come first-served basis.
- Specific software, documentation, and training materials as required.

Recommended Session Structure

- Experienced trainers will provide you with an agenda and schedule for their training. If you want to encourage peer-to-peer training as a way for people to pass on their knowledge even if they do not have training experience, it helps to discuss their plans ahead of time. Doing this will ensure they cover topics in a logical order, leaving enough time for hands-on activities and exercises as well as discussions and Q&A.
- I recommend making sessions as interactive as possible. For that to work, it helps to keep the group to a maximum of 10 participants, so each person gets enough opportunities to contribute, ask questions, and have their needs met.
- Start the day or training session with a round of introductions so that participants get to know each other. I am a fan of name tags or signs to help people remember names.
- If the topic of your session permits, launch into an exercise straightaway. This can be in the form of a discussion, gathering people's feedback on a statement of hypothesis, or having participants work in pairs or groups to solve a small problem. Most people love puzzles and challenges, so get them using their creative energy early on rather than spending the first few hours in a lecture-style approach.
- After the first exercise, teach some of your content, allowing participants to relate it back to the problem they solved at the beginning. Including plenty of examples, case studies, and real-life stories will make the content more memorable.
- At the end of each section of your training, include a hands-on exercise. When I teach data visualization workshops, I ask participants to put their laptops away and use pencils and paper for all exercises. It's a nice change for people to not be using a device with a screen; it reduces the chance for distractions, and they can more easily experience the lessons I teach about the use of color, the layout on a page, and the storytelling approach to data they may want to take.

- If you can teach your topic in an interactive way without a computer and instead get people up on their feet, using flipcharts, sticky notes, and colored pens, do so. Different mediums can engage participants in a very tactile form of learning.

- While exercises are a good way to break up theoretical content, adding breaks is also important. I recommend a short midmorning and midafternoon break, as well as a longer lunch break (45–60 minutes).

- In the afternoon, especially immediately after the lunch break, keep people engaged by adding more exercises and less lecture-style content.

- If time permits, have each participant present what they learned at the end of the day. Keep presentations to their key takeaways and consider assigning each participant a specific topic, so the last presenter will not get stuck with nothing left to say.

- Ask participants for feedback, either in person or through a brief survey afterward. Doing this helps you improve your teaching skills and supports you in creating a culture where feedback is a normal part of the process and is freely given and received.

Alternatives

- Replacing in-person training is possible if you cannot facilitate a session where people can attend and meet others. Running a full day of training remotely will be challenging, though, because of other distractions people might experience. If you need to teach people from afar, I suggest breaking the content into several units of 45- to 60-minute live webinars you can record and share afterward.

- Sharing written content, detailed how-to blog posts, and instructional videos are great alternatives you can use. Support these alternatives with a process for asking questions and receiving answers. This can be done, for example, through comment functionality on the platform you use.

Getting Started

This chapter contains six templates for events and activities you can organize for your community. These templates support the general guidelines and recommendations I outlined at the beginning of the chapter to help you start, grow, and develop your community. I encourage you to pick and choose those activities that make the most sense for your organization right now. Remember, not all of the responsibility for these activities should rest on a single person's shoulders. Success will depend on several people championing the cause and making things happen.

Take this chapter as a starting point for activities and changes you can make immediately. The most important thing to do is to begin. Then everything else will fall into place and you can gain momentum. Start by trying out one of the suggestions. I would love to hear from you with feedback on what worked and what did not work.

Chapter Eight

What Are the Success Factors for Your Community?

Whether you are in the process of establishing your analytics community or have not yet started, you need to understand some of the critical things that will make your community successful and something that persists for the long term.

In this chapter you meet the team from Jones Lang LaSalle (JLL) that manages a global analytics community operating the internal business intelligence services as well as analytics as a service for a number of their customers. In the following pages I share the lessons learned by the team at JLL, their suggestions for other organizations, and some examples of their work.

First up, meet Fiona Gordon from Sydney, who manages the global analytics strategy for JLL, a role in which she focuses primarily on tools, processes, and methodologies. As part of Fiona's job she is tasked with bringing together the various aspects of analytics across JLL, which include internal business intelligence and analytics as a service. At the time of writing, Fiona was in the middle of a project to bring consistency to every design aspect of visual analysis, dashboarding, and reporting across the business.

The methodology used by her and her colleague, Simon Beaumont, who is the Center of Enablement director, relies on well-designed change management processes and the implementation of design thinking to ensure everyone involved has a consistent approach and a shared understanding of the priorities, relevant tasks, and potential challenges. Through this methodology Fiona and Simon are accomplishing significant milestones along the way and working with everyone to improve and professionalize the analytics and data science processes used at JLL.

Specific Targets and Outputs

Having specific, measurable goals is helpful for making progress and for assessing performance. The same applies when it comes to establishing and growing your community. As you start bringing people together to work on projects and tasks, you likely will identify a number of processes and outputs that would help your organization.

At JLL, a past project to implement a consistent style guide for data visualization had challenges around the JLL palette and ease of use, so Fiona and Simon launched a fresh start for their Viz Guidelines, a comprehensive style and design guide for analysts across IT and the analytics teams in the various business units. Figure 8.1 shows the introduction section of JLL's New Viz Guidelines. Fiona and Simon understood that in order to be successful in building their guidelines, they would need more than a document. They also would require change management processes and a training program underpinning the implementation of this new approach to style and design. Figure 8.2 shows the old dashboard template and Figure 8.3 presents the new template.

On the surface, it might seem like a simple process to create a new color palette and layout guide for data visualizations and dashboards. However, this is no easy task, as branding, best practices, and scientific testing all need to come together in one place so that the results work well, can be easily understood, and will become part of the organization's brand identity.

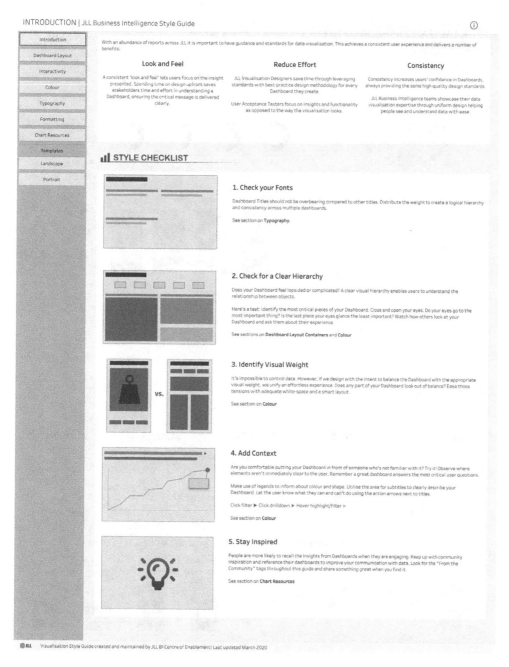

Figure 8.1   Introduction Section of JLL's New Viz Guidelines
Source: Jones Lang LaSalle IP, Inc.

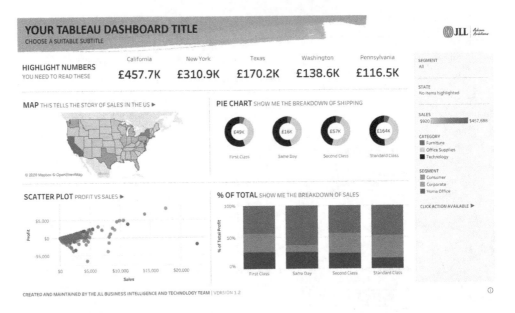

Figure 8.2   JLL's Previous Dashboard Template
Source: Jones Lang LaSalle IP, Inc.

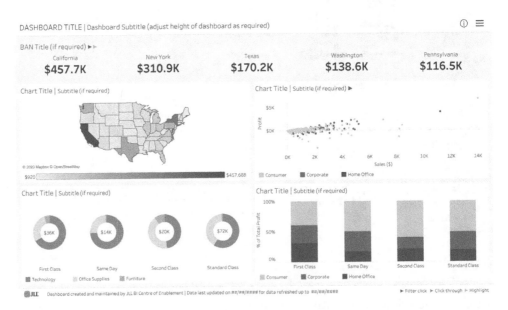

Figure 8.3   JLL's New Dashboard Template
Source: Jones Lang LaSalle IP, Inc.

For the team at JLL, having the specific target of creating the Viz Guidelines provided a tangible output, which in turn helped with these steps:

- Bringing together the right people for the project
- Identifying the necessary steps and milestones along the way
- Understanding the requirements across the business, including the different levels of change management required in different teams and business areas
- Creating a timeline for planning, design, testing, and implementation
- Setting out the overarching goals and priorities for the project in line with the company's strategy and priorities

Communicating Your Goals and Intentions

For any project or initiative, communication is key. Throughout my career, I have recognized the importance of clear communication in countless situations. Many issues, disputes, and failures can be attributed to a lack of communication. When setting up JLL's Viz Guidelines project, for example, which affects how people across the business design their work, it was important that the team communicate the project's intentions and benefits clearly to engage people early in the process and make the change management processes easier.

Fiona and Simon's team vision is to help people see and understand their data, and they are recognized as leaders in data visualization and visual analytics in their industry and beyond. They want their analysts to learn, understand, and apply best practices to ensure that any stakeholder can access information and insights easily and quickly. For this reason, utilizing and embedding best practices, backed by scientific research, is critical for their success and is something they consistently do throughout their projects. Doing this requires engagement with industry experts, technology vendors, and specialized consulting firms that bring the necessary expertise and research capabilities on best practices.

The team's project was fully endorsed by the marketing department as part of a brand refresh, which added additional credibility internally and alignment across the business. This support is necessary for change management and a successful implementation.

Following on from their vision, the team's goals for the Viz Guidelines included creating templates that utilize consistent formatting so that every report and dashboard follows a consistent approach, supported by best practices. A reliable and easily recognizable format and layout helps end users make sense of information that is presented and easily understand new data and insights as the presentation follows the same rules and patterns. Faster recognition and understanding will, in turn, make it easier to strengthen a data-driven mindset among analysts and to grow a data culture across the organization. JLL dedicates time to developing its employee culture: from standardization of the Viz Guidelines, establishing gamification programs to increase competency on strategic data platforms, and spending time to develop employees' technical and soft skills, such as how to provide and receive constructive feedback. JLL recognizes the importance of continuous learning, which requires investment of time, improving employee productivity and well-being. The hiring processes match candidates' values with teams not simply to ensure the best work product but to strengthen teams through their approaches to work. It is critical for teams to have opportunities to thrive. Producing reports and dashboards that all follow the same style and design guidelines also achieves a sort of branding for the analytics teams, and this branding elevates their profile with stakeholders.

The Viz Guidelines will be used by 400 to 500 analysts who work in the internal business intelligence function. The templates that come with the guidelines will lead to significant time savings. For example, senior leaders needed assistance to understand the impact of the COVID-19 pandemic on the business over a weekend. By following the Viz Guidelines, a visualization was created within four hours to help guide them through the process. Colors, structure, and interactivity were easily applied, with default workbook formatting removing the headache of standardizing font sizes and containers structuring a long-form layout in Tableau with ease. Without the template, refining the format would have taken significantly more time. Gaining efficiencies at the individual and team level is an important step in the overall process and will allow analysts to focus their time and effort on value-added tasks, additional analyses, improving their skills through training and development, and connecting with others across the team and the business. Reducing time wasted on repetitive tasks, such as formatting, layout, and choosing the right colors, fonts, and font styles means more time can be spent on carrying out sound analysis, testing hypotheses, obtaining feedback, and reviewing outputs.

Getting External Input

There are many opportunities with the #MakeoverMonday community and other virtual analytics and data visualization communities for outsiders to contribute feedback and expertise because the activities of these communities are all public and make extensive use of social media. The #Makeover-Monday leaders use this opportunity to work with technology vendors in the analytics industry as well as with organizations that need analytics expertise, so our community members can gain additional perspectives, learn from analytics and data visualization experts, and connect with subject matter experts in different industries. Getting this external input has been very beneficial to introduce fresh ideas, lend credibility to our activities and processes, and strengthen our community as well as the skills of our members.

When I spoke to Fiona, she explained that her team very consciously sought external expertise as well and applied scientific testing using EyeQuant AI software on the Viz Guidelines they developed. For comparison, tests were done on JLL's existing dashboards and reports, showing where people focused attention when looking at the information presented on screen. With the new design, the most important information was placed on those areas of the screen where people focus, ensuring they would consume critical information and insights faster and more easily than before and they would move across the dashboard in a more intuitive and natural pattern, guided by well-formatted and laid-out charts and text elements.

As Fiona said: "On a scale of 0 to 100, the score from the EyeQuant assessment measures how stimulating the design is perceived to be. Lower scores indicate a calmer design while higher scores indicate higher levels of stimulation. For data visualization, we want the User Experience to be calm, less exciting, only highlighting areas of interest." As shown in Figure 8.4, JLL's old dashboard template had an excitingness score of 34, according to EyeQuant AI tests. Figure 8.5 shows that JLL's new dashboard template achieves a lower excitingness score of 27, which indicates an improvement.

In addition to making their dashboards more effective, the team at JLL also wanted to ensure they are accessible to a wide audience. For the new color palettes, they chose colors that could be easily distinguishable by people with different levels of color weakness or blindness, with none of the colors too similar or too strong in contrast to cause confusion or misunderstandings.

These efforts were part of the team's mission to constantly improve their own skills and understanding as well as the guidelines they provide to the rest of the business.

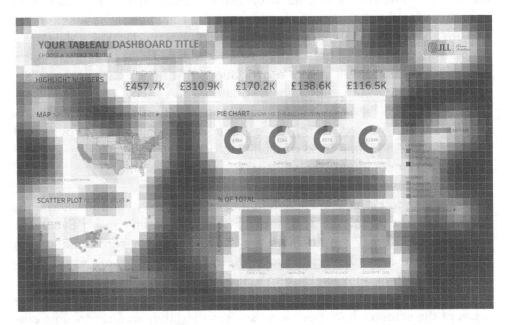

Figure 8.4   JLL's Old Dashboard Template
Source: Jones Lang LaSalle IP, Inc.

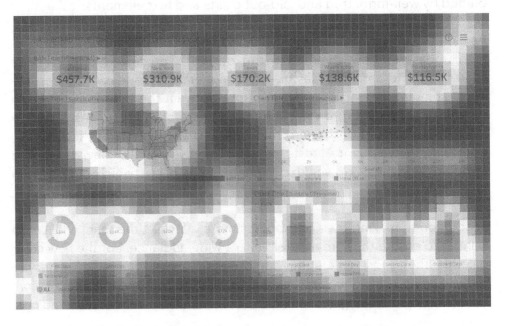

Figure 8.5   JLL's New Dashboard Template
Source: Jones Lang LaSalle IP, Inc.

Seeking external input from creative information design studio Set-Reset, who are experts in design, user experience, and digital communication, was critical for achieving Viz Guidelines that are practical, follow best practices, and provide a sustainable resource for the organization.

Driving Engagement in Your Community

Once you have gone through the steps of identifying clear targets and outputs and have communicated them to your community, seeking expert input along the way, how can you ensure that community members are getting involved and will stay engaged throughout the process?

The cross-organizational Center of Enablement, led by Simon Beaumont, had not yet been fully established for the business team when I spoke with Fiona. In the absence of such a formally established community, Fiona and Simon created training that was tested with small groups on Microsoft Teams and then formalized into an e-learning program. They identified champions across the analytics teams who would support them in their roll-out of the Viz Guidelines utilizing Yammer and Microsoft Teams.

They developed a roll-out strategy that would see the Viz Guidelines implemented across the business.

Their steps were as follows:

1. **Design training program.** Using the Viz Guidelines, devise practice tutorials for analysts to transform poorly designed visualizations into dashboards using the standards provided. Test the design on small teams to find where the program works and where it requires further information.

2. **Engage champions and train them on the new Viz Guidelines.** Turn them into evangelists who support the overall roll-out through their proficiency with the new design approach and their understanding of the underlying methodology and best practices.

3. **Communicate the Viz Guidelines from the leadership to the wider business.** Utilize a top-down approach that demonstrates leadership endorsement of the proposed changes and shares the vision of the team, together with milestones and next steps.

4. **Produce and publish e-learning modules for all analysts.** The team will provide online learning modules that bring the Viz Guidelines to life and make them applicable and actionable for every analyst.

5. **Test the Viz Guidelines in real-world scenarios, using existing business data sets and projects.** Selected people and teams will apply the Viz Guidelines in their daily work, using real data and projects and implementing the new design approach in their reports and dashboards.

6. **Embed the Viz Guidelines in JLL's Tableau Quest program.** JLL uses Tableau as its primary business intelligence tool. Fiona implemented a training program that uses gamification to encourage learning and development for analysts. Embedding the Viz Guidelines into the program ensures that the new branding of dashboards and reports is communicated through various training and data visualization challenges that form part of Tableau Quest.

7. **Go live for Viz Guidelines across the organization.** After successfully implementing the previous steps over the course of several months, the team will formally launch the Viz Guidelines as the new design approach for all reports and dashboards from the go live date.

This summary helps us to recognize the effort required to implement changes at a large, multinational corporation that is building a data-driven workforce to better serve its clients. Not all of us have projects of this size and scale, but we can all use the steps and approaches to inform our own projects.

Developing a consistent approach for tackling analytics and visualization projects, for driving data science initiatives, or for selecting a new piece of analytics software, is important and will pay great dividends in all the future work of your analytics community. The example from JLL shows that a measured and gradual implementation process that involves change management and carefully considers the steps necessary to get everyone on board is important to drive changes and improvements around data and analytics in our work environments.

I encourage you to follow the work of Fiona, Simon, and their team by connecting with them on social media (@VizChic and @SimonBeaumont04).

Chapter Nine

How to Set Up an Analytics Community

Having formulated your mission and goals as well as steps that support you in achieving them, the next step is to create a plan with milestones, targets, and dependencies.

Phase 1: Planning

With your mission and goals in place, it is time to make your community setup more tangible. Creating a plan, no matter how high level or detailed it might be, is a helpful approach to understand dependencies on processes, people, and systems and to see more clearly whether the structure, processes, and activities you have in mind can be achieved in the time frame you have given yourself. A plan also allows you to communicate with others more effectively on how community goals and activities relate to the larger organization.

As you build your plan, I recommend documenting the ideas you already are thinking about or have discussed with others. Here are a few steps you can go through to create your plan. Please note that the format depends entirely on what works best for you. Personally, I like creating these kinds of documents in PowerPoint so I have flexibility in the layout and design of the finished plan and can easily use corporate branding to give it a better visual appeal. You may prefer using a plan in Excel, perhaps even a project management tool, or you may write a document in Word.

To begin, create an outline with the different sections you want to cover. These include, for example:

- **Introduction**
  - State your community's purpose.
  - Outline what led to the idea of setting up a community.
  - Introduce the person or team leading the community and the initiatives you have planned.
- **Main section**
  - **List the goals of the community:** State what you want to achieve (e.g., professional analytics certifications for xx% of analysts; streamline reporting processes; automate data preparation, etc.).
    - Be as specific as possible in describing your goals. List specific processes or outputs the community will create or improve.
    - If training is a key goal for your community, outline what kind of training will be created and delivered, by whom, and in what time frame. List the gaps that currently exist and how this impacts the organization.
  - **List key activities:** Present a list of planned and potential activities to help people understand how the community will support individual members and the organization as a whole.
    - Will people participate in regular, recurring events, such as meetups or weekly challenges? If so, describe the aim for each event and what people will get out of the events.
    - Who organizes and runs the activities and how can others get involved? Knowing and stating these details will help to clarify the demands on individuals and show where additional help might be needed.
    - How can different departments or teams utilize the community via events and activities to make quick progress on a problem (e.g., via a hackathon) or to connect their analysts with those across the organization?
  - **Create timelines:** It can be difficult to plan and predict the various steps you are going to take ahead of time, but a rough indication of how you expect the community to grow and develop is helpful.

◇ Set targets for specific goals, particularly those that are time-bound.

◇ If you are planning regular events, list the dates and recurrences for these events.

◇ Add other milestones, such as reviews with community leaders regarding progress against targets.

• **Develop content:** To make the effort and contributions by every member in your community last longer, it is essential to consider how their outputs will be captured for others to access.

◇ Who can create written content, such as blog posts, guidelines, and how-to instructions?

◇ Where will content be published and shared? Is there a platform for content creation and sharing? How do people access it?

◇ Will you introduce incentives for content creators to encourage people to share and document their knowledge? What will these incentives look like, and how do people qualify for them?

• **List the next steps:** List the immediate next steps you are planning to take to get your community started or to take your existing community to the next level.

◇ Do you require specific approval for certain activities or processes?

◇ Who will be involved?

◇ What can people expect as a result?

The main bulleted items and questions will guide you to create a high-level plan which creates transparency around the community activities and assigns roles and responsibilities to those owning specific tasks or processes.

Example

At the time of writing, our #MakeoverMonday project joined forces with two other organizations—Operation Fistula and the Tableau Foundation—to plan a new initiative: Visualize Gender Equality. This initiative has the mission of harnessing the power of data visualization to highlight injustices experienced by girls and women. We went through a number of planning sessions to specify how we would start and run the project, which involves a monthly data visualization challenge run on the #MakeoverMonday platform, using a gender equality topic and data set.

Things we agreed during our planning phase included those discussed next.

Roles and Responsibilities

- The team at Operation Fistula was tasked with identifying suitable topics and data sets to use.
- The Tableau Foundation would support these efforts and promote the project to its network.
- #MakeoverMonday would provide the platform for hosting and publishing data sets, communicating with an audience of thousands of people, encouraging them to participate, and facilitating feedback webinars through the usual weekly process.

Timelines

- Data sets would be selected ahead of time and scheduled for three months at a time. Flexibility to change topics at short notice was built in to accommodate collaborations with nonprofit organizations that want to get involved.
- A launch date was agreed early on in the planning phase and communicated to those involved.

Events

- A "pre-launch" #MakeoverMonday live event was hosted at the 2019 Tableau Conference, where 1700 attendees worked on visualizing a data set about gender-based literacy rates. This event allowed us to test people's reactions to a gender equality topic and to start discussions about the initiative.
- Launch events were planned in several countries and cities around the launch date, utilizing existing Tableau User Groups. To support them, we provided a packaged presentation set and event template people could use to facilitate the in-person sessions.
- Virtual events, such as webinars, were also planned as they enabled us to reach a large audience with minimal resources and helped us cover different time zones through live and on-demand offerings.

Content

- The team at Operation Fistula planned several pieces of content to use throughout the year in support of the initiative. As the topics of gender equality and maternal health are their area of expertise, it was a logical way to share the workload.
- Gender equality in general is a topic that many people are aware of but do not have deep knowledge of or insight into. For this reason, creating relevant supporting content and messaging was even more important to ensure people are well informed when tackling different data visualization challenges.

Phase 2: Pilot

Whether you are planning to create a community for a department or for an entire organization, I recommend running a small pilot with a handful of people who will be involved in the future community as champions, technical experts, and/or influencers. Building a small team and going through a pilot phase will reveal some of the challenges and opportunities that the community will face. This phase is intended for experimenting, identifying the must-haves and the nice-to-haves while also understanding some of the people dynamics.

You probably already have some people in mind whom you want to involve in building the community. In Chapter 10, I portray a few community leaders whom I have met through my work and who contribute greatly to the analytics communities they are part of. Read their stories for ideas of what to look for if you are not quite sure yet whom to involve.

Whether the people who become champions for your community are highly technical, have years of business experience, or are passionate about creating effective and impactful data visualizations, there will be a role they can play in making the community a success.

Bringing diverse ideas, experiences, and backgrounds to the table is important so that your organization as a whole can be represented as much as possible and so that any activities and initiatives you plan are inclusive and open to participants from various departments and teams.

Meet with the people you have in mind and share your ideas. If you do not yet have a list of potential founding members, invite people to self-nominate to be involved through an internal messaging platform or an intranet page. As a group, discuss how you want to get started. My suggestion is to use an activity for people to participate in. Getting people involved through a regular meetup, whether it is a #MakeoverMonday–style data visualization challenge, weekly office hours, or a webinar series highlighting tips and tricks for analysis and visualization, helps to build momentum.

Running specific activities during your pilot phase allows you to test different concepts in a small group of people who are open to giving and receiving feedback and who have a shared interest in improving the setup of your program before opening it up to a wider audience.

- Is the room that is used for a weekly meetup suitable?
- Did you allow for enough time for people to learn something new and get answers to their questions?
- Does the webinar platform you are using work as intended across operating systems, browsers, and other equipment?
- Do you have interesting topics? Who is responsible for selecting topics for upcoming webinars?
- How will you allocate roles and responsibilities?
- What is people's availability like? Can they commit to the tasks you need them to do?

These are some of the questions you can explore during the pilot phase. There will be many more you can ask yourself and those around you, depending on how you want to build and grow your community.

How long should your pilot phase be? It depends. If you are planning to run weekly meetups and activities, I suggest you run the pilot for about two months, ideally three, so you can accommodate and experience different recurring events and see how they might impact the community. These events include:

- School holidays/term breaks and how they impact people's availability
- End-of-quarter financial results and reporting
- Urgent projects with high priority
- Releases of analytics software used in the organization
- Conferences and other events that demand people's time

In addition, running your pilot for two to three months means you have several opportunities to test your activities, events, and processes before inviting a larger audience.

If you want to run a shorter pilot phase, aim to have your activities with the pilot group occur more frequently to simulate the demands over the longer term.

Example

Returning to our Visualize Gender Equality campaign example, running a pilot phase was important for us as the team behind the initiative. Our first test was the previously mentioned #MakeoverMonday live event during the 2019 Tableau Conference. We used a data set about literacy rates in several countries with data available by gender.

We deliberately chose this topic, as literacy is a concept everyone in the room would understand and was not a topic that would make people uncomfortable. We wanted to see people's reactions to the topic and understand their level of engagement with social impact issues. The response was overwhelmingly positive from the 1700 people in the room as well as from those participating virtually.

The second step of our pilot phase was to present the initiative at Tableau's global sales kick-off, three weeks before the launch date. With a keynote presentation from Operation Fistula and #MakeoverMonday, we were able to reach an audience of around 2500 software sales professionals. The feedback was encouraging. People showed their interest by signing up for our initiative and reaching out to us personally to pledge their support and share their excitement about gender equality topics being brought to life through data visualization.

These two events, a hands-on data visualization challenge and a keynote talk, gave us the confidence that our ideas and processes were ready for the real thing in time for our global launch. Relying on existing systems, such as the #MakeoverMonday platform and schedule, helped our planning and testing phase and reduced some potential hurdles around tools and technologies.

Our next step was to look at the growth of the community involved in the Visualize Gender Equality initiative.

Phase 3: Growth

Once your community is up and running, with regular meetings and events, ideally even a structured or semistructured learning and development program in place, it is important to focus on growth and managing the ongoing development and evolution of the community. It is unlikely that everything will always go smoothly, so here I highlight some of the challenges you might encounter and the tools and milestones that you can introduce to keep members enthusiastic and motivated.

Potential Obstacles to Your Community's Growth

A community involves people, and people come with personalities, commitments, priorities, and different perspectives and ways of doing things. Disagreements are to be expected, and even the best-thought-out plan can be derailed. This is a given in any organization. By anticipating some of the potential challenges and finding solutions and alternative approaches, you will be well prepared for growing your community.

Below is a list of obstacles or 'speed bumps' you may encounter. Following that are some suggested tools that help you prevent or work around the challenges. At the end of this section I will share some of the challenges we expect for the Visualize Gender Equality initiative, based on my experience with #MakeoverMonday.

Challenges

- People may commit to participating in the activities you offer or to leading certain initiatives but over time their commitment fades and they do not follow through on what they promised.

  Possible reasons:
  - They have other commitments, priorities, and time pressures.
  - They do not feel engaged.
  - They feel overwhelmed or that they lack the right skills to make their participation meaningful.
  - They do not see how the community activities are relevant to their day jobs.

- There is not enough time to achieve the goals you or others have set, resulting in pressure and additional work for those involved.

  Possible reasons:
  - Poor planning that did not account for factors that could impact deliverables.
  - The work done in and by the community may not have been recognized by those setting the overall priorities, leading to additional requests in the time that was dedicated to working toward the goals.

- Lack of skills required to achieve the tasks and goals, which indicates a need for training and development.

- A change of management or leadership along the way results in a lack of support for the community as a whole or for specific initiatives and projects.

  Possible reasons:

  - Poor communication at the leadership level on existing priorities and activities, which leads to misunderstandings and a lack of appreciation for work that is currently ongoing.

  - The community was not visible at the leadership level, showing a missed opportunity. It is important to make the work visible at every level to avoid surprises and misunderstandings.

  - With new leadership there is typically the risk/opportunity of "Out with the old, in with the new," leading to wholesale changes in processes, systems, and tools. In these cases, I recommend communicating the value and achievements of the community proactively and identifying as well as communicating how the community will support new structures and approaches.

- Technical and data governance challenges arise. Every analytics community experiences such challenges at one point or another. People are left unable to access and work with specific data and/or software.

  Possible reasons:

  - There is still a noticeable divide between analytics in business units and the owners of systems and software, including the data environment in traditional IT. If this situation sounds familiar, you will need to create or improve processes that ensure your analysts can use the software they need to analyze data, find insights, and communicate them effectively.

  - Data should be governed in the organization. *How* it is governed depends on your strategy, structures, and the experience and methodologies of the people who are responsible for data. It is challenging when data governance is used as an argument against making data accessible to the people who need to work with it. Proactively address this topic by understanding the business questions being asked of the analysts in your community and creating clarity about the data required to answer the questions. Involving management and gaining approval at higher levels can be the most effective way to deal with this particular roadblock.

- There is a lack of appreciation for the importance of learning and ongoing professional development in the organization.

  Possible reasons:

  - Unfortunately, some organizations do not see the value in supporting their employees with learning and development opportunities. Instead, they expect employees to show up with perfect skills and knowledge. As long as such outdated views exist, it can be challenging to fully engage in a structured learning program and to offer various skill development opportunities to your community. But please be persistent because the individuals who attend and participate will benefit, even if that is not considered valuable at a general level.

  - Management might be concerned that investing in training their people could be a waste of money if those people subsequently find a better job elsewhere. In analytics, as in any other domain that experiences rapid development and growth, it is vital to keep people's skills current so your organization can compete in the market and make the most of its data assets.

Maintaining Momentum

- Introduce a recognition program.
  - Small rewards can make a big difference. If you have some budget for small gifts, such as vouchers, branded gear, or other items that people will appreciate, use it for small thank-yous and to motivate people.
  - Consider whether participation can become part of employees' formal goals.
  - Measure people's contributions (e.g., number of blog tutorials, number of questions answered on an internal forum or messaging page, number of templates created, events organized and hosted, etc.).
  - Recognize people for these contributions and make the recognition public as a way to thank them and to encourage others.
  - Use elements of gamification, such as levels or milestones people can achieve by participating, to inject friendly and fun competition into your community.
- Challenge your community.
  - Hosting a monthly or quarterly data analysis or visualization challenge that is open to everyone can get people out of their routines and reconnect them to the wider community.
  - Prizes can help to drive participation. Promoting the challenge ahead of time and publishing the results more widely in the organization afterward can be very motivating.

- Utilize showcases and demos.
  - ◆ It is beneficial to nudge people outside their comfort zones on a some-what regular basis so they recognize their own strengths and skills. Organizing a showcase event where people show some of their work is a great way to encourage them to participate, own, and be proud of the results.
  - ◆ In addition, a showcase event serves as an invitation to others to join your community as they can see what it is all about, who is part of it, and what people contribute.
- Hold expert talks.
  - ◆ Whether you set up a larger event or simply have a one-off guest lec-ture, bringing in external experts to speak about their specific topic can be highly motivating and can inject fresh ideas and momentum into your community.
  - ◆ There are many expert speakers out there. Reach out to several people so you can find the right fit. Communicate clearly to them what your expectations are, as many speakers are (and should be!) happy to tailor their talk to your specific audience and to help you with a call to action.

Example

What are some of the obstacles we expect to experience during the first 12 months of the Visualize Gender Equality initiative, and how do we plan to address them?

- Difficulty accessing, gathering, and sharing data
  The initiative relies on publicly available data that is granular enough for meaningful insights. The topic for the initiative can have significant data gaps where data is either not gathered or not reported, or it may not be disaggregated by gender.

  Solution: Gathering and preparing data early on will help us reduce the risk of not having comprehensive data sets to work with.

- Communication challenges when sharing gender equality topics
  Many participants are unlikely to be familiar with all of the topics we have prepared, and it can be challenging to communicate effectively with an unknown online audience.

Solution: To help participants to do their research and take responsibility for their learning, it is useful to prepare relevant content for each monthly topic that can be shared with the community and to make additional resources available for users so they can access more information.

- Showing meaningful outcomes while helping people grow their skills
  It is important for the initiative to result in data visualizations that can have a noticeable impact and that can support nonprofit organizations in shaping and sharing their message. At the same time, the mission of #MakeoverMonday still holds, and we need to ensure that aside from the specific gender equality topic, we maintain a focus on people's learning of data analysis, visualization, and communication skills.

  Solution: Continue with the proven process of feedback webinars, the highlighting of best practice visualizations, and the addition of blogs or webinars that teach specific skills and methodologies.

Phase 4: Development

Development and growth go hand in hand. To grow and develop your analytics community, focus on creating a structured learning and development program for the data professionals in your organization.

As you grow your community, you will naturally do more of the things that have worked in the past, such as activities and events, and you will likely involve additional people in managing and supporting the community. It is important to formalize processes and structures so they are easy to maintain. You want your efforts to be sustainable and do not want things to become "more work" as more people enter the community.

Formalizing Your Community Structure

When we think about formalizing structures, we often worry about introducing unnecessary bureaucracy. That is not the intention here. Instead of forcing your community in some sort of mold that stifles creativity, I suggest simply creating a few written artifacts that describe how the community operates, who is part of it, what it aims to achieve, how it fits into the organizational structure and strategy, and what its building blocks are.

Here is a list of structure-related items to consider formalizing and putting on paper:

- A description of what your community aims to achieve
- An overview of your community's structure
  - Community champions and their responsibility
  - Roles represented in the community
  - If applicable, the person, team, or department responsible for the outputs of the community.
  - Location-specific information if relevant
- Topics and areas of expertise covered by your current members
  - A skills matrix that people update with their skills every six months is a great tool for accessing the right experts in the organization for projects, tasks, and everyday questions.
  - Listing the gaps—the areas where the organization needs experts, but they are currently not yet part of the community—can help to recruit new members to your community.

I am a big fan of making things as automated as possible so they do not become additional work to worry about. Hence I suggest producing these structural documents or overviews in a tool that gives you the flexibility and convenience you need for updating them regularly.

Formalizing Your Community Processes

Before you start documenting the various processes around activities and events in your community, you may need to standardize them first. Processes such as project approval, software licensing, and assigning people to projects probably are done via existing processes driven by IT or business intelligence departments. Your community processes likely focus on learning, development, innovation challenges, events, and activities. I use this assumption for my recommendations on formalizing these processes.

Start by identifying all the processes that occur in your community. These might include any combination of those listed next (not an exhaustive list):

- Onboarding of new members
- Weekly activities, such as data analysis and visualization challenges
- Monthly activities, such as meetups and webinars

- Annual or semiannual activities, such as internal conferences and analytics showcases
- Internal training sessions
- Creating content
- Maintaining an internal community page (e.g., on your company intranet)
- Communication between community members

Some of these items will be easy to document as they are repetitive, following the same pattern with a set frequency.

However you choose to document these processes—whether you create detailed write-ups or high-level overviews—I recommend you use diagrams and simple flowcharts where possible to help people understand quickly how things work. A one-page overview for each process likely will be sufficient for any new community member to understand how they can participate and contribute.

Formalizing your processes by creating documentation that contains agreed processes and approaches is an important and helpful step for growing your community. Any method of signaling to the rest of the organization the importance of what you are doing, combined with a systematic approach that others can read about, will help you achieve greater understanding and acceptance of the work you and the community are contributing to the organization, even if not every task and output is immediately visible to those around you.

Creating a Structured Learning and Development Program

When you are ready to grow your community beyond its current size and activities, establishing a more formal skill development structure helps to reach more people in the organization. Large organizations and big corporations often have a formalized approach to learning and development, typically managed by the human resources department, where various types of training can be accessed. Whether they are online training modules or in-person classes, structures and processes exist to give employees the opportunity to increase their business acumen, technical skills, and leadership capabilities.

If you work in an organization with such a setup, you may be able to add modules about data analysis, visualization, and data science to the system.

Otherwise, you likely will have to find a way to create a system for your content and materials to make them accessible to your audience.

What to Consider When Creating Your Learning and Development Program

- What content do you already have that you can share more widely?
  - Start with some quick wins of making materials available to others. Ideally you have a platform that enables you to share content efficiently.
  - An index or inventory of available content as well as a list of things you want and need to create will help you plan additional materials.
- Does your organization provide access to formal in-person training classes that can be opened up to a wider audience?
  - Having a catalog of available training provides transparency and enables people who are interested in participating to seek approval from their managers.
- Do you have people in-house who can provide training? If so, have they gone through formal train-the-trainer education to support them in their teaching? Are they interested in focusing more on training their peers?
  - Having your own people become certified trainers (depending on the scale of your analytics community and your organization) is a great way to elevate the position of data and analytics in the learning and development program.
  - Some people may not realize their talent for teaching until they are in a position to test this out. Encourage them to become internal trainers if a position is available.
  - Internal, peer-to-peer training can save significant amounts of money as it reduces the reliance on consultants and external trainers.
- How many people do you want and need to train?
  - The number of people who may go through the training program, in whole or in part, will determine how frequently you run sessions and classes.
  - The facilities available to you, whether rooms for in-person training or virtual conference resources, will also impact the amount and frequency of training you can offer.
- What resources, time, and money are available for the program?
  - If you have the freedom to make your learning and development program part of the tasks that form your day job, you may be able to work on it consistently over a period of time without needing many additional resources. If you can involve others, even better.

- Otherwise, a budget will be required to access people's time and commitment for developing the program as a specific project.
- What timelines are you working to?
  - Depending on the goals of your community and organizational strategy and directives, you likely have fixed deadlines by which you have to achieve certain levels of qualification of data professionals, the development of training materials, and the like.
  - In addition, your involvement in the community is likely part of your own performance goals. Remember to consider the commitments required and the deadlines to stick to when developing your program.

Parts of Your Training and Development Program

I want to share a few suggestions of what to include in your program. These suggestions focus on content and in-person training sessions as two key components of your program.

Content

With every person who joins your community, you have another potential content creator. Do not hesitate to involve others in putting together training materials based on their experience and expertise. Focus on those who enjoy writing or creating such content and who are able to break down technical challenges, business concepts, and other topics into simple-to-understand descriptions, guides, and instructions for others to follow.

Examples of Content to Provide and Share

How-to guides
- Step-by-step instructions of how to carry out specific operations within analytics software and other tools used by the organization.
- Where possible, include diagrams and screenshots to make it easy for others to follow the instructions.

Manuals
- Make manuals available in an online library via links and downloads for those who prefer to access vendor manuals when facing technical questions.
- Ensure these are updated as upgrades become available.

Best practices

- A lot of things can be done with software and with existing processes, but not all those things *should* be done. To ensure community members are aware of best practices and follow them as closely as possible, make such guidelines available to everyone.

- Explaining the reasoning behind best practice recommendations makes them more likely to be adopted, so add descriptions into the documents.

Templates

- Depending on the software you use internally, templates may be available and widely used already. They are a good way to save time and to ensure that corporate standards are used where possible.

- Be open to feedback on these templates, and review as well as update them as required to improve their usefulness and ease of use.

Video instructions

- People have different learning styles. While some prefer to read step-by-step instructions, others do better when observing a person going through a process before following along.

- If you have the capability to create video content for teaching technical concepts, for presenting tips and tricks for using specific analytics software, or for sharing business topics, I highly recommend you do so.

- Find the right platform and system for creating and sharing video materials, ideally with a way to include external content you might have access to from vendors and industry experts via YouTube, Vimeo, and other systems.

Blog posts

- An analytics blog with different categories (technical, insights, how-to, updates, etc.) is a great way to open your program up to other contributors. A blogging platform helps to bring focus to people's knowledge and experience for everyone else to see and consume, whether people share materials only once or regularly.

- Provide some guidelines for blog posts (e.g., length of articles, formatting and style guides, how to submit, etc.), and have a plan for promoting the content internally once it has been created.

FAQ

- Regardless of your approach and system for collating people's most frequent questions and the answers, it is a good idea to put all those answers in one place in the form of an FAQ document.
- While FAQ documents may seem old-fashioned, hyperlinks and a web-based approach make them easy to maintain and update and, even more important, easy for users to search.

Tests and certifications

- Finally, consider creating specific tests for your users to complete so they can assess their learning progress and so the organization has a record and understanding of its people's capabilities.
- Develop the tests internally or have people complete official third-party (i.e., vendor based) certification exams.
- Having leadership support this level of skill development and assessment sends a clear signal of the importance of people's professional development to the organization.

In-Person Training

While online, content-based training gives you and the organization a lot of flexibility and the ability to reach many people at once, do not underestimate the importance of in-person training. In-person training comes with resource requirements, and it can be challenging to run classes regularly for a wide audience, so start small and build from there.

Here are some options you can consider, depending on your community size, culture, and geographical dispersion:

Externally facilitated classes

- Bringing in an external trainer gives your people access to industry and technical expertise you may not (yet) have in-house.
- Although they can have higher costs, external trainers typically are vendor certified. I recommend using only certified/accredited trainers, ideally based on recommendations from others.

- External trainers, whether you send people to a class offsite or have a trainer come to run an in-house session, likely also will be taken more seriously by attendees, as they understand the cost implications. These trainers often have more clout when speaking to your people.

Internally facilitated classes

- People with a certain level of expertise, specialist knowledge, and experience are great candidates for facilitating internal training classes, teaching their peers about different topics in analytics, communication, and data science.

- It is important to set out some rules and expectations around these training sessions to ensure the person teaching is known for their expertise, as peer-to-peer learning comes with its own challenges, including envy and refusal to participate. Hopefully your people will not experience this, but I recommend reducing the likelihood of problems surfacing by clearly stating the expectations around internal training.

Presentations

- Hosting members of your community and people from the wider organization to give presentations on specific topics during events or as standalone activities is a great way to highlight people's expertise, help everyone learn something new, and approach knowledge sharing in another way.

Webinars

- Webinars are engaging tools for bringing content to life. Rather than asking people to consume written materials or follow a video, webinars allow direct live interactions, either by voice or through written questions.

- Choose a webinar platform that allows you to record each session. Doing so will make the content accessible for others who are unable to attend but who would benefit from the interactive nature of a webinar, hearing familiar voices deliver content and share knowledge.

Promoting Your Program

Once you have a plan for your learning and development program and have put content and in-person training sessions in place and on people's calendars, it is time to promote the program and encourage participation. You will need to do a bit of internal marketing to create awareness for what you have created and to get people to sign up, participate, and become creators themselves.

Here are three steps you can take to share your program with your community and beyond:

1. Make learning and development part of people's performance goals.
   - Adding achievable and measurable goals into annual performance plans is a great way to nudge people to grow their knowledge and skills consistently and to give them a genuine incentive to participate.
   - Make the goals specific by specifying them, such as "complete basic training on statistical analysis" or other specific modules and events. Goals need to align to the person's role and responsibilities so they are relevant and motivating.
   - As a next step, add goals on creating content (e.g., one blog post per quarter) to people's plans to ensure that, as people increase their skills, they contribute back to the program and assist others in their learning journey.
2. Share content and news about your program on your organization's intranet pages and/or via an internal messaging platform.
   - Promoting your own work may feel a bit awkward at first, but do it anyway so people can find content that helps them.
   - Share the materials that exist and maintain them in a structure that is intuitive for the wider audience (e.g., categorized by topics, business area, technology, etc.).
   - Encourage others to help you promote training modules that particularly helped them.
   - If possible and feasible, introduce a bit of gamification with a rating system for content, an achievements system for contributors, and a way for people to find popular and effective materials.
3. Update content regularly to ensure it stays current with new software releases, accommodates specific strategic priorities and organization-wide projects, and has additions and changes as required.

- Updates are a good way to remind people about existing content and to drive conversations about training classes, upcoming sessions, and any requests for additional materials.

Summary

In this chapter, we went through a structured approach for identifying your community's "why," setting specific goals, then planning and piloting your community ideas before moving on to growing and developing your community, overcoming obstacles, and building your own learning and development program.

Setting up your analytics community from scratch or shaping, growing, and developing an existing community are exciting tasks to be involved in and will present you with interesting challenges to solve while building your own skills along the way.

Chapter 10 presents lessons learned from setting up communities. In it you will meet a few more people who have tackled the challenges of building analytics communities.

Lessons Learned

#MakeoverMonday has been a labor of love for me and is a project I care greatly about. When I started hosting the project, I put myself into it 100%. My enthusiasm led to a bunch of new ideas, changes, and updates to the projects and helped it grow. It also led to a lot of work for me, which I did in addition to my paid employment, in my spare time. There were plenty of lessons learned: what to do, what not to do; what to do more of, because it helped the community and the individuals within it; and what to do less of, because it exhausted me, took away the joy of running the project, or was simply not the best use of our time.

This chapter shares these lessons in the hope that they will help you avoid some of our mistakes as you embrace ideas and approaches that turned #MakeoverMonday into the successful global project it is.

Let's start with the mistakes I made.

How *Not* to Do It

The nature of #MakeoverMonday, as a project that runs online, is that we have participants across many time zones, cultures, and languages. If that was not challenging enough, all the interactions are online and mainly through

Twitter, where there are limited characters to express yourself. Those two aspects make proper communication very difficult, yet communicating our feedback to the participants is the most valuable part of the project for their understanding, the growth of their skills, and to ensure they come back week after week to practice and improve.

Unsustainable Levels of Commitment

When I first joined in January 2017, I tried to respond to every individual submission on Twitter with feedback, divided into multiple tweets to convey as much information as possible. So much was lost in the brevity of tweets, and I am convinced that many did not appreciate my bluntness, which was purely out of necessity, because adding extra words for politeness would have required even more tweets.

When I recognized that my feedback did not always reach the participants, I started to take screen shots of their visualizations and annotated them before sharing them on Twitter. While this made *What* I was suggesting they change in their visualization much clearer, there was no room to explain the *Why* behind my suggestions. And if people do not understand why I give them certain feedback, their learning will suffer.

Finding a Better Way to Give Effective Feedback

A few months into the year, our project's growth had attracted attention from BrightTALK, an online webinar platform, and we were offered a channel for webinars. After a few tentative first webinars hosted by BrightTALK, we came up with the idea to create a feedback webinar called Viz Review, where we would review people's work and comment with suggestions.

The beginnings involved a bit of trial and error, as was to be expected. Our initial approach was to copy people's images from Twitter into a slide deck and then go through the slides during the live webinar. This was not a bad idea, but preparing the slides each week was a lot of work. Then we experimented with sharing our screen and simply going through the Twitter feed of submissions (those that included the hashtag #MMVizReview, a way for people to indicate they want feedback).

This worked much better. It required no preparation for the weekly webinar, and we gave our feedback on the spot, as we navigated through people's visualizations. Once we gained confidence in the process, supported by people's feedback and continued participation, we also added live demos into the mix. We downloaded selected visualizations on the spot and made some of the changes we suggested to show that simple tweaks could make a big difference to how effectively the information was communicated. We also started to build visualizations from scratch with the data of each weekly challenge to show what could be created in 10 minutes when you break the data down into simple, focused charts and apply best practices through the process of designing a visualization.

Experimenting with Different Platforms

Aside from BrightTALK, we were also approached by data.world, a platform where people, groups, and organizations can host data. The team at data .world were excited to support our project, and we started moving our data sets from OneDrive to data.world. It was great to have a very accessible central place to upload spreadsheets and supporting documents and to track some of the usage.

We started hosting all our data on data.world in January 2018. After growing tired of the limitations of Twitter, we decided to use data.world's discussion feature to collect all webinar submissions in one place. We still wanted to keep the webinar as an opt-in process, where people have to specifically request webinar feedback, because it is not necessarily something everyone wants to participate in.

Why Moving to Another Platform Did Not Work Out the Way We Expected

Using data.world for these discussions was a conscious choice away from the noise of Twitter, but after several months, we found that data.world also had its limitations and impracticalities.

- On data.world the discussion was public and open, but it was limited to those people who came specifically to participate. This excluded the wider public, other analytics and visualization experts on social media, as well as the potential for nonparticipants to get inspired. While many people still shared their work on Twitter (in addition to data.world), their exposure to potential employers and other collaboration opportunities, based on the quality of their analysis and visualization work, was greatly reduced.

- The discussion feature also had one major limitation: There was no threading feature. This means that comments appeared in chronological order, which made it very difficult to have detailed discussions about particular visualizations.
- We also found that people did not follow the process we asked for, which resulted in slow loading times of the discussion pages as everyone embedded their dynamic and interactive visualizations. The webinar was cumbersome to run, as we wasted precious time waiting for links and visualizations to load.
- And finally, having data.world as our main platform while still managing parallel conversations meant we had to manage and keep up with two different platforms. Doing so created extra work and sometimes frustration.

How We Fixed It

For us, #MakeoverMonday is a project that is all about improving the way we visualize and analyze data, one chart at a time. It's also about the growth, development, and learning process of our participants, giving them the best chance to grow their skills and have fun while they do it.

Leading this project means we learn all the time. When we find something does not work, we figure out a way to address it.

Unlike in business, we do not use any formal approaches or methodologies because #MakeoverMonday is mainly business as usual for us. We are always willing, though, to learn, adapt, improve our processes, and optimize the way we engage with our community. I think it is absolutely critical to not attempt to set anything in stone, in the hope that it will be perfect forever. Communities are fluid; they change, they grow, they shift focus as priorities change. With those requirements comes the need to be flexible. It can be hard to invest a lot of time into making something great only to realize it is not so great and more changes are needed. Yet if we let our egos get in the way of true progress, our communities cannot thrive.

How Did We Solve Our Platform Issue?

We went back to Twitter as the single platform for engagement. We still host all our data sets, supporting documentation and links to original visualizations and articles on data.world because it makes it so easy for us. However, we no longer engage in any discussions on the platform and instead ask our participants to use Twitter.

The benefits of this change for the participants are:

- Increase the visibility of their work.
- Engage with people beyond our community.
- Have an open and accessible platform for sharing.

Did this fix all our problems? No. Twitter still has its limitations and even two years after moving away from the data.world discussion feature, people eagerly post their work there. The majority of people have, fortunately, moved to Twitter and joined our weekly conversations there.

Other Examples of Overcommitment

Aside from the effort we put directly into the day-to-day running of #MakeoverMonday, we also found other ways of overextending ourselves. This is something we really realized only with hindsight.

Too Many Events

In the first year of running #MakeoverMonday with Andy Kriebel, we ran a number of live events to bring people together around the idea of analyzing and visualizing data on a specific topic in a short time frame. We ran events in Paris, Berlin, Munich, London, Amsterdam, Sydney, San Diego, and Las Vegas and held additional local events. By the end of the year, we noticed how much stress the traveling and organizing had caused us.

Our lesson learned was to limit the events we did to those that we could include in trips we had already planned and to offer virtual introductions to the community. This meant that other people might host an event at their location. We would simply dial in via video to say hello to participants, introduce them to the project and how it works, then hand the event over to the people on the ground. This approach made our lives much easier, reduced our travel, and allowed us to virtually meet many more people than we would otherwise have, all from the comfort of our offices or living rooms.

Not Setting Limits

In my entire time of leading #MakeoverMonday, I often simply failed to set limits for myself. As a community leader, I recognize that doing so is my responsibility. However, I also see it as a common risk for people who have a mission they are passionate about. When you start, grow, and develop a community, you are helping others, and it is all too easy to give too much of yourself. Yes, being on the receiving end will be great for your community members, but setting boundaries is essential so you can build structures and processes that are sustainable and that will continue to help others.

Over the years I learned how important it is to be clear about my commitment to the project. These are some of the reminders I give to myself:

- What is my goal and why am I running this project?
    - Remembering that I want to help people improve their skills helps me focus on the essential steps I need to take to achieve that goal.
    - Reminding myself of the good work that happens in #MakeoverMonday helps me get through the more difficult times.
- What time commitment am I willing to make?
    - Especially with social media interactions, setting a clear time limit can be difficult.
    - I focus on the value-added activities I can complete, such as running our weekly webinars, providing constructive feedback, planning specific campaigns, and creating additional learning content.
- What is the most important thing to do right now?
    - When things get very busy in my day job due to speaking engagements and travel commitments, I need to scale back my #MakeoverMonday involvement to a minimum.
    - For those times, I focus on the essential tasks: publishing data sets, creating my own Makeover and blog post, running the feedback webinar, and highlighting the best visualizations of the week in a recap blog post.

Overcommitting to Creating Content

After we started using BrightTALK as a webinar platform, there seemed to be an endless number of topics we could turn into helpful webinar content for our community. While I enjoyed coming up with ideas and figuring out how we could best educate our members on topics ranging from mapping geospatial data to talking about the UN sustainable development goals to tackling design challenges, the result was a lot of extra work that I had not actually planned any time for. The main challenge is that these additional commitments creep into downtime and personal time, which then leaves less time for family life and even plain and simple relaxation and recharging from daily work life.

My solution to this problem was *not* to reduce the amount of extra content we provide; I think the resources are incredibly helpful, and I want to continue creating them for our community. Instead, I made a conscious effort to work with experts who would present their topic of expertise on our channel. People in the community as well as experts from the outside get a platform with well over 10,000 subscribers while we receive curated, high-quality content that injects new knowledge and ideas into the community.

Drawing on experts is something I would strongly recommend as a way to continue the learning process, to support you in creating new content in a sustainable way, and to bring new ideas to your community.

Who Are the Right People to Lead Your Community?

Every community, group, or team needs a leader. Often these leaders emerge naturally, but in a business context they are typically established through a formal process. With most analytics communities growing from an idea and developing into much bigger initiatives, it is important to involve the right people to lead the community through the different stages.

How do you find the right leaders for your analytics community? How can you identify them? How can you ensure that the quiet people are not overlooked?

Examples of Leaders in Analytics Communities

I have been fortunate to meet many great leaders in the communities I am part of, focusing on data, analytics, and data visualization. These leaders are not necessarily the ones everyone sees and hears. Rather they are those who do good for the people around them and lift them up.

The two women profiled here have made their mark on the community in their own unique ways, shaping conversations, helping people, building community structures and processes. Here is their perspective on leadership in analytics communities, combined with their story of getting involved.

Maria Brock

When I spoke with Maria, I asked her what "community" means to her. For her, community is like a family: individuals who are bound together by constant support and admiration for each other. Family and community both consist of selfless individuals who share resources and use their skills to uplift those around them and improve the quality of their friends' and colleagues' lives.

Maria became a part of the Tableau community as a Tableau Student Ambassador in 2019 and has given much of her time to help others learn and achieve. Her impression of the Tableau community is that it is bound together by a mutual goal: to share knowledge generously with one another to help fellow developers gain answers. Whether through the forums, user groups, or Twitter, people will always find someone who is willing to take time out of their day to help them find solutions and answers.

Moreover, people can make friends in the Tableau community, because participants are eager to connect with each other and promote each other's work, break boundaries, and create thoughtful discussions and projects to encourage others to use their skills for good. "The community pours into you so you can grow," says Maria to sum up the community she has become a part of.

When I asked what motivated her to give back to the community, Maria told me it was in part to return the many favors she had received during her initial period of learning, absorbing, and finding answers. Initially she felt hesitant about being a student among so many professionals, worrying that she may not have anything meaningful to contribute. What she realized after she started teaching free Tableau workshops at her college was that she could help grow the Tableau community among students. She wanted students to access the same resources that she was able to, so she started sharing content among the student ambassadors. Ultimately she built a website, www.thetableaustudentguide.com, where students and those new to Tableau could find all the resources the community provides. Hearing students tell her how these resources have helped them is the best validation she could get.

I had the honor to watch Maria progress and flourish in the community and emerge as a leader. I asked which part of her mindset, work ethic, or attitude toward others helped her to be successful.

Maria believes that leaders emerge through their work in helping others and sharing resources happily and without expecting anything in return. When a leader is needed, it is the individuals who step up and build the community who are recognized for their leadership traits. Being a leader means taking responsibility for others and for your organization and being willing to put in the work to help others grow.

Leaders serve the community, they do not take for their own gain.

Sarah Burnett

I have known Sarah for a number of years through the #MakeoverMonday community and appreciate the experience and professionalism she brings to her work. Sarah has worked in data-focused roles in the banking sector for many years. In her own words, she describes how she got started in working with data:

> Numbers have always interested me. I can remember quoting figures as a young child. "Mum did you know there are 3 million people living in New Zealand and 1 million of them live here in Auckland."

> I completed a Bachelor of Management Studies at university and naturally found my major in information systems. My first job was in the coffee industry as a marketing manager. But data found its way into my role. I recall building a Microsoft Access Database listing all the cafés in New Zealand. I actually had to manually scrape the White Pages on the only computer in the office to do it. The telesales team thought I was crazy. A while later I worked for them in Melbourne, Australia, targeting cafés again. This time you could buy a CD-ROM with the data on it, and it contained the size of the cafe based on the number of seats. I was able to cross-reference the postal codes with the sales reps' areas. Mind-blowing stuff back then.

On top of her current role, Sarah is a Tableau Social Ambassador and co-leads the Singapore Tableau User Group. She is a regular speaker at events in the Tableau community and beyond and is engaged with local university programs to share her knowledge and advice. Being creative and finding different ways to share knowledge, engage the data analysis and visualization community, and teach others is part of what Sarah does and what she enjoys. She encourages people to stand up and tell their own stories, and she gives them a platform to do so.

As a leader in the community that I am part of as well, I asked Sarah what she thinks are some important leadership qualities to have.

"Having an open mind, taking constructive feedback, and making sure it's fun." Sarah suggests there are many ways to help others achieve success, and it is important to keep things fresh and interesting, especially in a fast-paced industry like data analytics.

How Communities Find Their Leaders and What Challenges the Leaders Faced Along the Way

The London-based chapter of Data+Women aims to promote and celebrate the achievements and success of women working in the data industry and gives them a platform to share their knowledge and experiences. Anyone and everyone is welcome to attend Data+Women events, including men. Speakers at events are women sharing their stories. The group was started by Emily Chen, who saw the gap in the local community, which featured several tech and data-related user groups but none focused on women in the sector.

The group holds meetups twice a quarter and is aiming to increase the frequency to provide more opportunities for people to connect, learn, speak, and share. A typical meetup has between 50 and 70 attendees; technical workshops have a smaller audience who are, however, more specialized in their skill set and the skills they want to learn.

From Emily's initial idea and the support from Sophie Sparkes, who handled many of the event logistics, the community grew. At the beginning of 2020, a new leadership team formed to manage the large community, run more events, and involve other people who were interested in participating.

Louisa O'Brien, Natasha Kurakina, Caroline Yam, and Archana Ganeshalingam, who are part of the leadership team at Data+Women London in addition to their full-time work and other personal commitments, shared that it can be challenging to build and grow the community in the local market in London, which has a high number of existing meetups, interest groups, and communities. They aim to balance the desire to connect people while being mindful so people do not become overwhelmed by social events. The women told me they focus on developing a meetup agenda that ensures the time attendees commit is used most effectively. An additional challenge is that each event needs to stand out among the many local events on offer, which requires strong speakers, interesting content, and a well-rounded agenda. The team wants to ensure that each event attracts new people so that the community continues to be diverse, resulting in new connections, fresh ideas, and healthy discussions.

Over the course of a year, the leadership team of Data+Women London aims for a program of events that is meaningful for their existing community and also leads to growth. Obtaining feedback from community members is an important way to address the needs around knowledge sharing, learning, speaking opportunities, and current market topics. The program of events and the way in which the events are run still need to represent the brand and culture of the Data+Women London community so attendees have a positive and inclusive experience at every event.

While these are challenges the team needs to tackle, Louisa, Archana, and Natasha told me that listening to others is a key factor in getting things right. So they listen not just to one another but also the wider community and align this feedback with their overall mission. They hold regular review meetings after each event to debrief on the things that went well and those that could be improved next time. The women told me they enjoy being part of a group of like-minded people, all women, and working with them on building this community. They are passionate about the network they are building and want this passion to come through in the events they organize. They want the overall feel of the events to be fun and welcoming and to align with the group's brand and mission. Each meetup also has the goal to inject new ideas, new topics, and learning opportunities for attendees. And of course each meetup is an opportunity for the leadership team to learn as well, to see if attendees enjoyed the event and to challenge themselves to create a fun atmosphere where people feel welcome and can be themselves in a relaxed environment.

In regard to the leadership team and the process through which people can become part of it, Caroline Yam told me that formalizing the process of finding new people to join the team had a very positive effect. The existing leaders developed an application and interview process that aimed to align applicants with the mission and core values of Data+Women London, so that people become involved for the right reasons. Caroline and her team were able to form a team of six women from diverse backgrounds and ages who will drive the activities of the community, support events, identify speakers, and help members form many new connections while learning, sharing, and engaging with one another.

Community Champions and the Impact They Have

Every community needs its champions to get started, to grow, and to thrive. The situation is no different in data and analytics communities, and there are many passionate leaders who create and nurture communities related to various topics. Bringing their expertise, experience, and typically a desire to help others means that community champions need to find a balance between giving and setting boundaries to ensure their efforts are sustainable and do not become a burden or a reason for burn-out.

To get some perspective on the enjoyable aspects of being a community champion as well as how to find the necessary distance and balance that keep the joy of giving to others, I spoke to Sam Parsons, a leader in the data visualization community. Sam is based in the United Kingdom and inspires those around him with his masterfully designed visualizations on topics ranging from music to sports, from agriculture to politics. Sam's journey from starting to explore data visualization in Tableau to becoming an expert in visualization involved a steep learning curve and fast progress due to consistent practice, his openness to feedback, and his willingness to explore diverse topics and approaches.

Author: Sam, you are a key contributor in the data visualization community, particularly in the UK, and you are also engaging with people virtually at a global level. What encouraged you to get started with being involved and giving to the community?

Sam: From the outset of my Tableau journey I was lucky that the company I was working for transitioned to using Tableau. It was the training I attended that opened my eyes to the wider community that Tableau has to offer and that it was different to anything else I had encountered up to that point. There was a clear emphasis on

	celebrating others' work, being selfless with your own time to help others, to share your ideas and work—it was clearly a healthy community that I just had to be a part of. From there I wanted to be involved, I created my Twitter account and started to share my work.
Author:	You started by getting involved in a few community initiatives then quickly developed your own style, a distinct approach to design that expanded your skills. How did this happen?
Sam:	This really was an organic process. At the time when I started using Tableau and discovered the wider community I was predominantly working in spreadsheets, reporting KPIs and data in table format. I found using this new tool to be a creative release for me, it allowed me to reconnect to my design roots (I studied design and manufacture at university), and so naturally I wanted to learn it as quickly as I could. The community is so rich with different initiatives and projects to get involved in, all designed to help you practice your own skills and also receive feedback on what you have created. This is a wonderfully enriching process and a very safe place to try things.

The first project I tried was #MakeoverMonday. When I started all I was interested in was learning Tableau, and I was happy just to be able to put a dashboard together that technically worked. I then started finding the community blogs, mostly technical blogs, tutorials on the different bespoke charts you can make if you applied a bit of mathematics to Tableau.

At first, I don't mind admitting, this spooked me a little—thinking to myself, "Would I ever be able to create something like that?" or "I've no idea how to even start with this!" Then slowly as I read through the blog tutorials, I started to gain an appreciation of what people were doing. I came to the conclusion, if they can do it, then why can't I? So I decided to start using #MakeoverMonday to try making new charts that I had never made prior to using Tableau.

I made the decision that in order to accelerate my learning, I couldn't always call upon help from the community; I had to learn by myself what Tableau was doing. This might sound the opposite to being community driven, but I knew I had to learn the tool in the way that best suited me. I was concerned that calling in help from the community would result in those people fixing my chart issues, without me really understanding why it wasn't working in the first place. I was then more than happy opening up my work for feedback to the community and as part of the #MakeoverMonday feedback process. As time went on, I was learning more about best practices and formatting tips and tricks. I then became better equipped to make Tableau do what I wanted.

I constantly take inspiration from the community, but I try not to re-create what others have done; I want my work to be my own and done in my own way. This is the reason I very rarely invite feedback when building a new visualization. This helps to keep my visualizations distinctly mine, I am the sole person that decides when I feel best practice is best applied and when you can loosen those ties a little, for more creative and storytelling effects.

Author: You are a community champion, helping people online as well as driving the ongoing growth and development of the community in your organization. How did you go from "participant" to "community leader," and what do you think are some of the characteristics or approaches that helped you along the way?

Sam: How I went from "participant" to "community leader" was a mental shift that also coincided with a change of job to a new company. The first part of that mental shift is attributed to the positivity of the feedback loop from the online community. Having people celebrate your work is enormously reassuring and validating. For me it helped me feel that I had found a community where I belonged and I was on the right track with my own skill development. In short, I was finding my confidence.

The second part of the mental shift was that I felt my views were just as relevant as others' [views]. This really helped me contribute more of my own views and give feedback directly to others. I try to be active within the online Twitter community, highlighting things I like and celebrating others, in the same way I found community members did with me when I was starting out.

Around this time I was also in the process of changing jobs and starting at a new company. I was brought in as a visualization specialist for my own team, but I quickly found the company community was very inwardly focused; I was the only person that was active in the wider online community. I made contact with the internal community, offering my help and expertise. I put myself forward for teaching others about data viz best practices, presenting in internal Tableau Clubs, and helping new analytic teams. I joined in on weekly analytic meetups to discuss how to improve our internal community and then offered to help support and run our internal Tableau Club.

What I think made this a success was an enthusiastic approach, being willing to give your own time to the community and also understand that while it is not necessarily part of the job role you get paid for, it will bring its own benefits.

The other element and possibly the most important is having an appreciation of the community work that has been done prior to your involvement. I found adopting a soft approach worked really well. I first took the time to be a participant in the internal Tableau Club, to see how it is being run, to understand if support was needed and appreciated, before getting more involved.

Author: What makes you keep giving?

Sam: The memory of how the community treated me when I first joined them. I can clearly remember conversations with people I was looking up to and the time they were giving me. I want to follow that lead and be able to give back to the community in the same way. To do that though I had to sit down and have a think on where I could add to the community, what would be useful, and where my own expertise could really be of benefit to others. I started my blog—ReflectionsInDesign.com—as a space to write about anything that I wanted, content that I was interested in. I wanted to talk about design in general, elements that are not as widely discussed in our data visualization community and nevertheless still important. The feedback has been wonderful; knowing you are helping others really does make you want to continue doing more and keep giving.

Author: What suggestions do you have for growing the next generation of community champions? How do you identify the right people and then help them, nurture their talents and give them responsibilities?

Sam: I feel there is not a single answer to this. On the one hand identifying the right people should be easy; they should be the ones putting their hands up.

The others are people who are clearly talented but don't put themselves forward. Try to build those people up. Encourage and congratulate them on smaller wins. This will build their self-confidence, so you can encourage them to become more active in the community. Ultimately it is down to the individuals. A lot of people are hard to convince of the benefits of being more involved with a community, maybe they feel they are too busy to devote the time to it or maybe their personal goals are aligned elsewhere. Which brings me back to my original point; there has to be some self-drive within the individual to want to improve and learn. If that is there, then it is easy to direct and show them the benefit that the community pathway will bring.

How to Assign Roles and Responsibilities

Once you have identified the right people to involve in establishing an analytics community in your organization, how do you assign roles and responsibilities? In this section you will learn how to find the balance between playing to your strengths and moving outside your comfort zone. Doing this ensures that your community members can challenge themselves and grow while also finding ways to contribute in line with their key skills and adding value in the process.

Alteryx User Group

First, meet Joe Lipski and Paul Houghton, two members of the organizing team behind the Alteryx User Group in London. Joe and Paul have been hosting many meetups and have supported the local Alteryx community in London for several years, so I asked them how they approach leadership within the team.

The Alteryx User Group is aimed at new and existing users of Alteryx, people who want to learn more about how to use the analytics software for their own work and who want to improve their technical skills while meeting like-minded people. To achieve this, the team around Joe and Paul organize four to six meetups every year, hosted at different venues across the city, typically by an Alteryx customer or partner. Participants come from a variety of businesses and industries, making for a diverse group at each meetup, with a range of experiences, questions, and needs.

One key goal for the user group is to help people improve the way they work, as Alteryx can speed up data preparation and analytics processes significantly. Enabling data analysts to become better at data preparation and analytics results in many people having a much more enjoyable day at work because many menial tasks are automated, and they can focus their efforts and expertise on high-value-added activities. With the growth of Alteryx in the analytics market, the user group grew as well. Meetings are typically attended by 50 or more people.

How does leadership work for the team?

Usually a meetup is planned mainly by one member of the organizing team who chooses the direction, including speakers and agenda. She or he is then supported by the rest of the team, who complete various tasks required to make the event a success. Between setting up registration pages, managing invites and communications, checking in attendees on the day, and ensuring that food and beverages are provided, there are several moving parts to take care of. The work is distributed evenly, and each team member has the opportunity to step up and lead a meetup throughout the year.

When it comes to the content of the user group agenda, Joe and Paul told me that some people can be reluctant to share their stories because they consider themselves to be novices and feel they have nothing of value to share, expecting everyone in the room to have a very high level of expertise. The balance between nudging people to step outside of their comfort zones and empowering them to play to their strengths does not apply just to the leadership team. It also matters when working with the members of your community.

To address the challenge Joe and Paul identified, they started a new concept, which reduces the expectations placed on any particular speaker to give a 30-minute presentation. Rather this shift focuses on small and specific topics. A series of talks, each only five minutes in length, encourages a diverse range of speakers to share their expertise relating to a specific tool in Alteryx, how they use it, how it works, and how others can apply it to their use cases. Lowering the barriers to speaking at a user group by setting up a number of short and sharp talks means the team expects to see many new speakers emerge.

Finally, Joe and Paul told me that about half of the people at each meetup are new to the group. Welcoming so many new members to their community each time is a great way to engage the wider analytics community in London, across businesses and industries, and serves as an exciting platform for many more people to share their story.

St. Joseph's University

The final success story of analytics communities comes from the world of academia, more specifically, St. Joseph's University in Philadelphia, Pennsylvania. I spoke to Kathleen Garwood, assistant professor at the university, about the community she and her students have built over the years.

Author: Kathleen, how would you describe the community that has formed at St. Joseph's around analytics and data visualization?

Kathleen: The community is self-run and motivated. While the concept of teaching a lesson in visualization (using either Excel or Tableau) was added into the master's curriculum in 2012 and later to the undergraduate curriculum in 2014, the community itself reaches far beyond the classroom. Currently, we have 15 graduate and undergraduate student tutors who hold open labs from 9 AM to 9 PM every Monday and also create lessons and presentations that they hold in a wide variety of classes. These students also create dashboards for different departments, supporting a variety of St. Joseph's initiatives. The tutors also take part in expanding their own portfolios, for example, through the #MakeoverMonday project and by creating visualizations for nonprofit organizations.

We have monthly data build lessons run by alumni (a network of 20+ volunteers) who talk about best practices, how visualization has changed the workplace, and who show students some basic techniques, tips, and tricks all while also networking with one another. monthly, we host the Philadelphia Tableau Users Group allowing the students, tutors, and alumni to network with companies who are using the tool and looking to hire young practitioners.

Author: When did it get started and why?

Kathleen: The group was initiated by Senior Corey Jones in December 2015 as a way for students to meet and work on data visualization. He was supported by Tom O'Hara (senior) and Amar Donthala (grad student), and he asked me to consider being the academic advisor. Corey started with the concept of monthly presentations, which quickly became biweekly, with more than 30 participants per event. Topics included how to build visualizations as well as concepts of dual axis, color choices, design, formatting, and filtering. Corey, Tom, and Amar put together 10 different presentations for the spring of 2016.

The initiative evolved and despite Corey and Tom graduating and leaving the university, they continued to stay involved and engaged as alumni, encouraging us to set up a #MakeoverMonday lab in September 2017, with the goal of having both undergraduates and graduate students work to help students, who range in level from beginner to adept, get started in data visualization.

Author: What are some of the processes, events, and tools you have in place that help people get started and stay engaged?

Kathleen: It is important to note that St. Joseph's University is an academic setting. Therefore, while the initial goal was to start a Tableau drop-in lab, it quickly became evident that students were looking for help with several parts of the process (Excel, data cleaning, R, Python) as well as considering several tools (Tableau, Qlikview, Power BI). So we tried to make sure that every Tableau tutor also had other skills they could help students with. The use of Tableau is prominent, but the lab is structured to help people build their data visualization skills.

Allowing students to have opportunities through holding the monthly Philadelphia Tableau Users Group (TUG), hosting competitions (Men's basketball analytics competition Fall 2019), promoting students for service (Kinney Center, Arrupe Center, Finance Department), and working with colleagues in varying disciplines, especially marketing and sports marketing, has helped ensure the foot traffic has more than doubled since the lab opened. Meanwhile, several department grants have included students providing visualization skills to create dashboards for varying projects.

The lab is a starting place. It allows faculty to drop in and get help planning lessons while also being a space they can send their students to for help with their class assignments and projects. The students work together and learn from one another. The students who participate most enthusiastically often become the tutors for the next year. The collaboration and efforts have advanced the lab and also the course offerings throughout the business school. Once a student gets started, they often see that using visualization can help them with assignments beyond whatever they initially came for.

Author: How important is your industry network for helping you grow this community and introducing new ideas for the students?

Kathleen: Starting with Corey, Tom, and Amar, who have stayed connected with the student community, all of the students who have worked in the lab stay in touch and support the tutors and me in the lab. They are available when we get stuck doing advanced visualizations for the varying grant work as well as university visualizations as they advance.

At each St. Joseph's University TUG, multiple alumni come to support the presenters and then stay around and answer students' questions. While I can facilitate the location and invite students, the actual presentations are run by the alumni. Because of their enthusiasm and talent, we have more than 40 students, staff, and alumni in attendance every month.

Author: What is the feedback from the students? How do they report benefiting from this community and all the work you do?

Kathleen: My students get good jobs and compete in markets that far advance their new graduate status. What they are learning in the classroom on business intelligence and analytics is advanced. When they start visualizing data, they see a bigger story and start to tie in the skills they are learning in different classes to help them complete their data story. It takes time for them to find their voice, and once they start, everything they have been working on comes together. Because of the alumni network and the monthly Philly TUG, I have the opportunity to talk to many alumni on a recurring basis and see the advancement and changes as they progress. I think the foundation provided by this group truly enhances prospects for the students that choose to take advantage of it or who truly enjoy data visualization.

PART III

PART II

Chapter Eleven

Where to Go from Here

In Parts I and II of this book, I took you through the reasons why an analytics community can benefit your organization and shared many examples, ideas, templates, and suggestions for establishing your own community. In this final part, I want to focus on the future and help you sketch out what you can and need to do next to get started from scratch or continue your existing work to grow and develop the people in your community, increasing their knowledge and skills and building a truly data-driven culture across the entire business.

Your Roadmap

As you move forward from today, it will be much easier to get to your destination if you have a plan with steps and milestones that will help get you to your goal. The same is true for many aspects of life, whether sports, academia, or personal challenges.

In my conversations with people from different organizations who are actively managing communities and initiatives around data and analytics, what resonated most with me was that all of them had a plan to follow rather than leaving success up to chance. To develop your roadmap, take stock of where you are at right now and review the goals you have set out for your community.

Are there specific tasks and projects you and the other members will have to accomplish by a certain time? If so, make this the basis for your roadmap.

Remember Fiona and Simon from JLL? They were working to a specific time-line and had clear steps they wanted to accomplish along the way, such as training key people on their new Viz Guidelines before testing them with selected stakeholders and adding them to their company-wide gamified training and certification program. Their overall goal was to embed new branding and colors into every report and dashboard produced by hundreds of analysts across the organization. With a global enterprise the size of JLL, an ad hoc approach would simply not work. Having a clear roadmap helps Fiona and Simon keep the project on track, helps them report on steps completed, and gives them a template and methodology for future projects.

A roadmap can also become a nice visual guide that is displayed and communicated to a broader audience. Why not produce a well-designed time-line with each milestone on a poster that is displayed in the office or shared online within the team, the community, or the entire business to communicate the work that is happening?

I recommend assessing your current targets and goals and identifying what can be achieved—realistically—within the time you have. Such planning plus prioritization will be important when new requests come in and compromises may need to be made. Keep your roadmap as the plan that guides your community activities, communicates to your stakeholders, and shows everyone what to expect and where things are heading.

What Does Your Future Community Look Like?

If you are currently at the very beginning of building your analytics community, you probably have a few ideas of what you would like to start with. If your community is already up and running, you may see certain areas that you'd like to improve or new projects you want the community to tackle. The responsibility should not rest entirely on your shoulders. Without knowing the situation at your organization, I will simply continue to address you as the key person.

There are so many different directions people can take their community development into, so I will share some of my ideas for #MakeoverMonday and how we went about implementing, changing, and optimizing our work along the way.

#MakeoverMonday grew very organically throughout the years. There was never a grand plan or big vision but rather small steps we took, new ideas we implemented, and little nudges that we used as inspiration for changes and improvements. When I think about the future of #MakeoverMonday and how I looked at this over time, it was always a question of: How can we make the project better for our participants? This question guided me and was a useful way for assessing whether changes would lead to improvements or not.

When we started hosting webinars for our community, we decided to use them as the key feedback mechanism. Over time it became apparent that this was a critical new component in the project and one that helped people learn, improve, and understand how they could get better at visualizing and analyzing data.

As #MakeoverMonday is a free project, none of our ambitions was commercially driven. We were excited to see participation numbers increase and the subscriber base to our webinars grow. We saw this as indications that we were helping people and reaching a larger audience who would, we hoped, get a lot of benefit out of participating in the webinars, the weekly challenges, and perhaps even live events.

Within an organization, your targets likely will be much more specific than ours, because your success will be measured based on the value you and the community add to the business and how well the analytics community supports and furthers the strategy of the entire company. In my view, there are two steps you can take for moving forward.

First, set your targets and identify the different tools, resources, and steps you need to get there. Such a roadmap will likely involve people, processes and technology, and probably also a budget to some extent. Second, take stock of what the community is already doing or, if you are just starting out, what exists already that you have access to. Get together with your community champions and even a wider group (you are the best judge of whom to involve here) and brainstorm how the existing resources can be used to achieve your goal.

For us at #MakeoverMonday, our goal has always been to improve the way we visualize and analyze data, one chart at a time. When we were invited to set up a free and full-scale webinar channel on BrightTALK, we used that offer to develop content that would support our mission. And over the years, we certainly delivered on that mission! Our goal is one that will never be completed. Yes, we will help many people along the way to become better, to become experts, and to work with us in helping even more people. But our work is never finished. We will continue looking for ways to engage our audience.

What do you and your community have available to you? Is it access to great analytics software that you can get every community member trained and certified on? Do you have someone in your organization who brings strong statistical expertise? Do you have a very open-minded creative department with people keen to get involved in improving visualization designs so they are more engaging and help you tell better data stories?

If you can identify the resources available to you today, you can map out the path forward more easily and get started immediately without raising requests and obtaining approvals first. Instead, make a start and deliver a number of outcomes that add value to your organization. Use these deliverables to strengthen your position when it comes to negotiating future requests.

What Are Your Goals?

By now you have sketched out a rough roadmap with a high-level plan of what you want your future community to look like. Consider the next examples before I move on to setting goals, so that we are all on the same page.

Community Vision and Roadmap

Example 1: Building a New Community

You have identified the people you would like to involve in your community (e.g., data analysts, data scientists, data visualization experts, and business stakeholders with subject matter expertise).

You want to start bringing people together on a regular basis to foster exchanges between members, so that those without data analysis experience can gain knowledge and skill in working with data and using analytics software, and those with data expertise can expand their business knowledge.

Within the next six months you want to establish a schedule of regular meetups, organized and run by community members. You also want to increase visibility on the skills that exist in your community.

What your roadmap could look like:

1. Step 1: To bring people together, identify a handful of topics and themes that can be used for your events. In parallel, set up a skills matrix (e.g., in a shared spreadsheet) where you can track the skills, expertise, and interests of community members.

2. Step 2: Work with your community champions on deciding the right format of events. Great ways to get started are user groups, focusing on analytics software used in your organization, or meetups related to specific topics, such as data visualization best practices for the financial services industry or data science applications for developing game strategy in soccer.

3. Step 3: Set up your event. The guidelines in Chapter 7 will help you with the details.

4. Step 4: Decide on the dates for the next three to four events for the next six months to ensure you have enough time for planning and preparation. Doing this helps with communicating details well in advance and with finding speakers and inviting your audience.

5. Step 5: Execute. Each event becomes a milestone on your roadmap. During each event, engage with attendees to encourage them to participate in future events and initiatives. Share the skills matrix with them. By doing this, you will have a more comprehensive picture of the talent available internally by the time you reach your six-month milestone.

Example 2: Running a Project with Members of Your Community

You have an established analytics community. It might consist of a handful of people or already have dozens of people and several teams involved.

People in your community may have similar skills (e.g., data analysts) or a diverse range of skills coming from the business departments, data science, data analysis, and data engineering.

You have a (big) project that needs to be completed. Examples include: transforming existing Excel and PowerPoint-based reports into interactive dashboards using any of the leading business intelligence and analytics tools. Alternatively, your project might be to develop an internal training program around data and analytics for new analysts and those joining the company in other areas. You have six months to complete the task.

Your roadmap could look like this:

Step 1: Identify a project leader and decide on the scope of the project.

Step 2: For your report transformation, you will need to take stock of everything that exists. Who will be participating in the project, and what skills do they bring? I recommend going through and recording the skills people have as well, so everyone can play to their strengths and there are opportunities for learning and development.

Step 3: Develop a project plan with clear objectives and timelines. As part of this exercise, you can produce example before-and-after reports so everyone knows what to aim for. Is the goal to simply replicate existing reports in another tool, or will you be changing report format and functionality as well?

Step 4: Divide and conquer. Divide the tasks between everyone on the project in a logical and fair way to ensure workloads are balanced, people's abilities are aligned to their tasks, and tasks can be completed within the allocated time. Remember to consider the demands of people's day jobs.

Step 5: Track progress. Check in regularly with the team to ensure that tasks are on track to be completed in time and to the level expected and required. Having milestones in your plan will also help communicate the progress to your stakeholders internally. Regular updates on the progress will allow you to support the change management process.

Step 6: Manage expectations. Ensure that communication about any timeline slippage is proactive and timely.

Step 7: Complete the project and take time to celebrate. It is important to finish the project and to celebrate the achievements of the team and to acknowledge people's contributions. Take time to do this.

These examples only cover the actual task of changing the reports, not the process of managing the change internally. The idea behind the examples is to outline what projects could look like for your community and to suggest steps that will form part of your roadmap.

Setting Goals

For the specific tasks and projects in your community, you will need to set goals, targets, and timelines. What about the community as a whole though? What goals do you have for the community you are establishing and growing in the organization (or in the public domain)?

You may start with a specific task in mind, such as the ones suggested, but I am certain that you have goals for your community. It is worthwhile to make those goals specific, to write them down, and to communicate them as part of your community's mission.

Is your community there to turn the organization into a truly data-driven enterprise? Do you want everyone around you to become an analyst and to become proficient in working with data?

Those goals require a strong focus on training and development as well as change management. Helping people understand the benefits of being data literate and obtaining analysis skills, paired with an understanding of how to communicate results and insights effectively, will greatly support you in aligning everyone toward a common goal. Doing this will also give you a better chance at moving in the right direction.

Is your community there to focus on very technical projects, such as implementing a new analytics software across the organization? Is your community actively involved in establishing data science capabilities? Do you have data engineers supporting a significant project to migrate data from a legacy database into a new, purpose-built analytics platform?

These projects and initiatives will require specific technical skills and are a great opportunity for people to get involved. One goal for the community here could be to bring the systems owners (likely the IT department) closer to the people who use and work with the data. There is also the opportunity to make data science a bigger part of your analytics community if it was previously not well represented.

The process of thinking about and setting the overall goals for your community is important and should also be a fun aspect of being a community leader or champion. Doing this is vital to ensure that the goals are aligned with the overall direction of the analytics department or teams and the direction of the organization as a whole.

I recommend you engage with senior leadership early in the process to gain their support for your community projects and activities. Doing so will help you obtain the information you need to align your community goals to the targets that need to be achieved at the organizational level. Hopefully your organization is already planning to transform into a data-driven business, opening the doors for training and development initiatives for your people as well as welcoming the introduction and development of analyses, interactive reports and dashboards, and the use of data for every decision that needs to be made. When you work on this alignment, securing the resources you need to continue growing and building your analytics community, offering more training opportunities, adding tools that make people's lives easier, bringing advantages to the organization as a whole, and making analytical work more effective and efficient become easier.

Going to the level of the individual community members, it is also a good idea to align the goals of the community with those of the individuals who are part of it. Communication and negotiation is required to align people's managers with your community objectives, but the process is worthwhile to go through to ensure that people's contributions are recognized and rewarded.

To connect people's individual goals to those of your community:

- Set specific targets for each person around their contributions over the year. Targets may include creating content (blogs and articles for your knowledge exchange portal), presenting their work to a wider audience, and participating in specific projects.
- Align people's expertise with the needs of the business (e.g., by offering them tasks, such as teaching and training others; developing training materials, such as videos and manuals, or having them create guidelines that can be applied across the company for all data visualization projects).
- Incentivize people for their contributions through monetary and non-monetary rewards (e.g., sending them to specific conferences, to training courses they are interested in, or offering small rewards, such as books).
- Ensure the performance review process considers all the contributions an individual has made to the community, especially when their day jobs may involve a number of very different tasks. If people's normal work and their participation in the analytics community are separate, it is important to take all the work into account, not just what is in their job description.

Documentation and Building a Knowledge Portal

Documentation

Many of us cringe a little when the topic of documentation comes up because it is often an unloved part of a project or initiative. I argue that documentation is a very important aspect of the work of your community. And I do not necessarily mean the very specific documentation approach to requirements analyses and build specifications. By "documentation" here, I mean keeping track of the work you and those in your community are doing.

Here are some questions that can guide you in developing documentation, such as notes, short articles that you will share internally, etc.:

- **What are some of the things you experimented with and how did they turn out?**
  Document these trial-and-error phases in a way that helps you review what worked and what did not and share your lessons learned with others.

- **Who is part of your community, and what is their expertise?**
  Setting up a skills matrix where people can list and rank their own expertise (e.g., on a scale from 1 to 5, beginner to expert) and indicate what they are interested in and what they would like to learn will give you an excellent resource for finding the right people for projects, activities, and events.

- **What are some of the recurring themes, tasks, and activities in your community?**
  When observing your community, what things happen regularly? What are some frequently asked questions? What are the repetitive processes that potentially could be improved and automated? Document and track these activities and processes as well as common issues to develop the necessary improvements and guidelines for people, so they can help themselves and see the need for improvements on their own.

In the #MakeoverMonday project, we started documenting standard responses for recurring questions, which we will eventually publish as an FAQ document on our project website. At the time it means we need to make a small effort to track commonly asked questions and save them as well as document our answers. In the short term, we can use the already documented answers to respond to ad hoc queries. Over time we can build out a comprehensive FAQ document. Trust me, taking this approach will help you deliver constructive and considered responses to various questions from new members and experienced participants alike.

Building a Knowledge Portal

In Chapter 4 you heard from Pippa Law about the knowledge portal her community built at a large UK bank. It takes time to build up these resources, and the only way to get there is to get started. I recommend doing exactly that. Taking some of those lessons learned from Pippa and her team to get set up.

You likely already have a number of articles, solution documents, and diagrams that you can use. A worthwhile project is to bring everything together in a consistent structure on a platform that scales with your needs, allows collaboration, and can cater for multiple contributors so you or the portal administrator does not become the only person who can add content.

A variety of platforms are available, whether open source or proprietary, that you can use for managing content, collaboration, and members. Besides needing to choose the right platform for your community, you will also need processes for managing the portal and the content.

Consider these questions when setting up your knowledge portal. This is not an exhaustive list. but it will get you started with thinking about the processes and quality checks you need to apply:

- How do you ensure articles and answers that are posted are correct?
- Who is responsible for quality assurance?
- What kind of content do you want members to post?
- And with what frequency?
- If there is a need for specific content, how do you communicate with your community and send out a call to action?
- Who are the content contributors?
- Will everyone be involved or only selected people?'
- Who can access the content? Is it publicly accessible to the entire organization?
- How do people interact with the content? Can they comment on articles and indicate how helpful they found them?

If you work in a smaller organization, implementing a full-blown knowledge portal might not be feasible for budget and capacity reasons. That is not a problem. Likely you will have to spend more time identifying and developing the right processes that help give people access to content and resources on a shared drive or through specific sharing processes in collaboration tools. But it can be done.

A centralized knowledge portal that is accessible to a large number of people will help you make processes and projects more efficient and will lead to significant time and cost savings over time.

Automate

A very important lesson learned through our #MakeoverMonday project was to automate everything that could be automated. With the weekly structure of the project, there were plenty of opportunities to make processes more efficient. There are, unfortunately, limits to how much certain processes can be automated. If you get stuck in a situation where further automation is not possible, I recommend building templates as much as possible.

Machines cannot take over human interactions; an automated message cannot replace your weekly, biweekly, or monthly meetups, training sessions, or user groups. To make the whole project of your analytics community sustainable and manageable, put together templates and standard processes that you can communicate to others easily and quickly.

To help you with some ideas, here is a list of processes we have in the #MakeoverMonday project and how we handle them:

- **Collecting visualizations and data sets**
  We use a collaboration tool called Quip where we have a table listing each week of the year. In this table we have five columns: the week of the year, the date, the link to the data set on our data.world project, the link to the article/visualization and data source, and finally a tick box for when the week is completed. Project leaders can access and edit this document and collect all the information for each week before publishing the data.
- **Publishing data**
  Each week we publish a data set on our data.world project and our website. To make this a consistent and simple process, we follow three steps:
  1. We set up a new data set on data.world, following a template from which we copy the standard text and then update the relevant hyperlinks and descriptions. We add the data set, the visualization, and any additional documentation.
  2. We simply copy and paste the information from the Quip table into an existing table on our website, makeovermonday.co.uk/data, before updating that page and making it public for everyone to access.

3. We send out a tweet to our community, including the picture of the week's visualization to makeover, a link to the data page on our website and the #MakeoverMonday hashtag.

- **Reviewing visualizations on the Viz Review webinar**
  Participants who want feedback can register for the weekly webinar on our BrightTALK channel. The registration and email process is fully automated through BrightTALK. Including the #MMVizReview hashtag in their tweet and being preregistered to the webinar means we will put participants on a list, which we create through Tweetdeck (a tool to manage Twitter). This list is what we utilize during the webinar, going through submissions in chronological order. Creating the list is still a manual process of comparing tweets to webinar registrations, but given the limited time of the webinar and the number of requests for feedback, we have to reduce the number of reviews to a manageable level.

- **Weekly recap blog**
  At the end of the week, we publish a blog post with our favorite visualizations created during the week. We have created a template for this blog on our website. Using the template means we need to update existing objects, such as images and hyperlinks, but the effort is minimal compared to starting each weekly blog post from scratch.

Templates and automation will go a long way in supporting your efforts to build and grow your community over time.

Delegate

It can be fun to start a project on your own and see and be recognized for your achievements. Creating an analytics community in an organization, no matter its size, will not be feasible if you try to do all the work yourself. A community consists of more than one person. So let me encourage you to delegate work and tasks as well as involve others in coming up with ideas as much as possible.

It took me many years to learn this lesson, and I am still working on getting others involved, but the payoffs are very worthwhile. Let others bring their own talents, perspectives, and enthusiasm to the work you do collectively as a community of data professionals working to achieve your goals and those of your organization. The diversity of thought and approaches this brings is something no one can accomplish on their own.

The skill matrix I mentioned earlier will help you find the right people to delegate tasks to. In addition, make sure to communicate regularly and openly with people so they can put their hands up for things that need to be done.

When Andy Kriebel and I wrote our book about #MakeoverMonday, the lessons learned from the project, and how to approach data visualization and analysis tasks and projects, we had to split up the work in the most effective way. We quickly settled on who would be responsible for which chapter; we did not have any difficulties deciding this, because we agreed to play to our strengths. Some chapters were naturally a better fit for Andy, while others were a better fit for me. We also recruited people from our network to proofread certain chapters, ensuring quality content and accuracy. And then we had to manage the reviewers, making sure that the reviews would be completed in time so we could meet the deadlines given by our publisher.

Not every delegation process will be smooth and easy, so create clear visibility for what needs to be done, what is involved (as far as it is known), and what skills are required to achieve it. Doing this gives people the opportunity to pick and choose from the available tasks and projects and assign themselves to work that interests them and suits their skill set.

Ask for Help

Delegation is a way of asking for help, but you may need input from others outside of your community and even outside your organization. Do not hesitate to reach out to your wider network in your industry and beyond to get input, answers to your questions, and their perspective on the project you are working on.

In my conversations with the people you have met in this book, I have found time and again that people who work in data and analytics roles are very happy to share their expertise, ideas, and knowledge in order to help others avoid some of the challenges they've faced and to enable others to learn from their mistakes and find the right solutions for their organization.

Having a mentor or even a friend who can be a sounding board is extremely valuable. I have a small number of people whom I seek input from regularly on how to tackle certain challenges and improve the work I do with the #MakeoverMonday community and beyond.

Above all, asking for help will give you a very good chance at keeping things fun and enjoyable, even when projects get difficult or when work becomes stressful, because it redistributes the work, so the responsibility does not rest with you alone. Building a strong network internally, supported by external connections, will give you the foundations that will help you to continue leading your organization's analytics community and building it from small beginnings into a movement that drives outcomes, aligns to the overall strategy, and helps your people see the value of data and data-driven decision making.

Conclusion

When I developed the concept for this book, I wanted to share my excitement and enthusiasm for analytics communities to inspire you to become part of one yourself or to start one in your organization. I did not want to stop at ideas and inspiration, however, and wanted this book to be a guide with many examples, practical approaches, and real-world workable templates and instructions for taking action right now. I am confident that the previous chapters have given you some ideas you can implement in your work environment to bring people together around the shared interest in and passion for data and analytics.

It is my hope that using these recommendations will help you create a stimulating and open environment for learning, experimenting, sharing, and teaching and that this brings your analysts, data scientists, and developers together in new and exciting ways.

I also added suggestions that help you address potential challenges and problems, so while I hope you will not need to do so, I am sure you are well equipped to tackle any issues with a few extra tools in your belt now.

Communities thrive on the connections we form, and I invite you to become part of the communities that are out there in addition to starting your own. I would love to hear from you. You can find me on Twitter @TriMyData, on LinkedIn, and via the #MakeoverMonday website, makeovermonday.co.uk.

I wish you all the best for building, growing, and developing your community, and I hope you'll share your stories and successes with me.

—Eva

Index